SAMURAI
WARFARE

D1536198

Below: Osaka castle at sunset.

Dr Stephen Turnbull

SAMURAI
WARFARE

ARMS AND
ARMOUR

Cassell & Co.
Wellington House, 125 Strand, London WC2R 0BB

First published 1996
This paperback edition 1997
Reprinted 1999, 2000

British Library Cataloguing-in-Publication Data
A catalogue record for this book is available from
the British Library.

ISBN 1-85409-432-7

Distributed in the USA by
Sterling Publishing Co. Inc.,
387 Park Avenue South,
New York, NY 10016-8810

Designed and edited by DAG Publications Ltd.
Designed by David Gibbons; layout by Anthony A.
Evans; edited by Michael Boxall.

Printed and bound in Spain by Bookprint, S.L., Barcelona

CONTENTS

CONTENTS

PREFACE

The history of samurai warfare is the expression both of an ideal and a reality. The ideal was, and to some extent still is, an image of the noble warrior, sword in hand, fighting a single combat with a worthy opponent as part of a co-ordinated battle, planned and executed according to a meticulous and honourable tradition. The reality is often that of a surprise attack by night, followed by a clumsy style of warfare exemplified by the burning of fortified buildings and indiscriminate slaughter, in which all hope of tactical precision is cast to the wind.

This work will tackle the issues thrown up both by the ideal and the reality, and will demonstrate that in spite of the very evident evolution and development through the centuries, certain aspects of samurai warfare remained remarkably consistent, in particular its élite nature and the predominance of the small group as the basic fighting unit. Developments in army organisation, weapon technology and communications will also be studied in detail, and related to the wider picture.

The book is organised in three sections. Part One traces the historical development of samurai warfare from the earliest times to its peak in the Sengoku Period, the 'Age of War' in the sixteenth century. Part Two is an in-depth study of samurai warfare at this time, tackled on a topic basis, including battles, siege craft and naval warfare. The final section consists of a number of selected case studies, where the points raised in the preceding chapters are applied to historical situations between the years 1560 and 1650.

Many people have been helpful in the writing of this, my tenth book on samurai. I am delighted that Richard Hook has joined me to translate into superb artwork the new material on armour, castle design and heraldry which my researches have uncovered over the past seven years. I am very grateful to Tim Newark, the editor and the publishers of *Military Illustrated* magazine for allowing me to re-use some of the material from my series of articles entitled 'Samurai Warfare'. I also thank all those who have allowed the Japan Archive picture library to photograph their collections of prints, book illustrations and armour, thus enabling me to produce another book on samurai with nearly all new illustrations. I thank Dunstan Gladthorpe in particular. All the photographs used in this book are from the Japan Archive collection, except for a number of rare items from Christie's, which are gratefully acknowledged, from Fukui Museum in Japan, and from Rolf Degener's print gallery in Düsseldorf.

My study tours in Japan were kindly facilitated by several individuals. Eiji and Nahoko Kitajima helped with arrangements, and Mr Masayoshi Itō proved to be a very helpful guide to the Nagashima area, while Mr Kazukata Ogino once again entertained me at Nagashino. Mr Satō of the Asakura Museum at Ichijō-ga-tani helped with the identification of names from the Anegawa screen.

Above all I would like to thank my dear wife Jo, without whom none of this would have been possible.

Stephen Turnbull

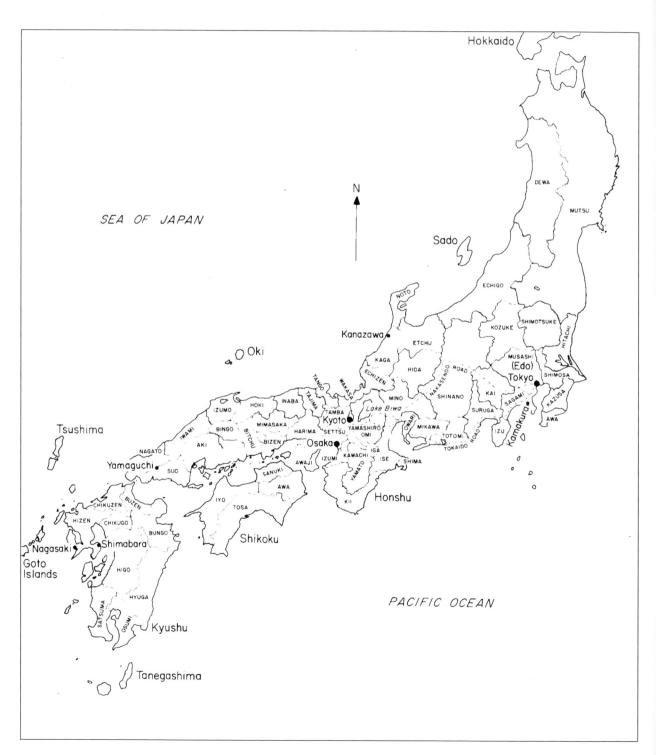

Part One

THE DEVELOPMENT OF SAMURAI WARFARE

Chapter 1
EARLY SAMURAI WARFARE

The Ancestors of the Samurai

The word 'samurai', which is commonly used for all varieties of ancient Japanese warrior, actually signifies the military élite of old Japan, a knightly caste who commanded armies, and also led their followers into battle. Their military and political skills eventually enabled them to control civilian governments, developing, through almost constant civil warfare, a set of military techniques, traditions and skills that may be called samurai warfare. The nature of the samurai ensured that the history of samurai warfare involves two very important aspects: the military activities of the group, through strategy and tactics, and the military prowess of the individual warrior. Both factors reached their peak of development in about 1600, which saw the culmination of a century and a half of inter-clan fighting known to historians as the Sengoku-jidai (The Age of the Country at War).

The two aspects of the needs of the group and the demands of the individual are in constant tension throughout samurai history, and find expression in several ways. At times there is a conflict between warrior élitism and the need for the deployment of large numbers of soldiers. At other times there may be a personal dilemma between pragmatism and the demands of samurai tradition, as exemplified by a fondness for heroic single combat, which was retained long after such activities had become anachronistic.

Such appeals to samurai tradition came from a nostalgic ideal of earlier samurai behaviour. This chapter will examine how these ideas were formulated, and will show that, although later generations may have regarded them as a romantic but impracticable ideal, the traditions were based on the experience of actual battle situations. The main sources for these accounts of early samurai warfare are the epic war chronicles called gunkimono (war stories). They will be used here to illustrate how samurai warfare began, and how it developed until the time of the Gempei War at the end of the twelfth century, when the samurai established themselves as the real power in Japan.

The word 'samurai' first appears about the middle of the tenth century, but by this time Japan already had a well-established military tradition. The foundations of the Japanese state were laid during a series of conflicts whereby one ruling house, the Yamato, achieved dominance over its rivals. The Yamato rulers were the first emperors of Japan, and during the latter half of the seventh century an incident occurred which was to threaten the Yamato hegemony, and ultimately lead to the emergence of the samurai class.

The Emperor at the time was Tenmu, who reigned from AD 673 to 686. A succession dispute threatened his rule, but was settled by Tenmu by a dramatic use of military force, including the skilful employment of cavalry. Tenmu quickly made his position sufficiently secure to be able to take the momentous step of attempting to disarm all his opponents. From 685, therefore, it became illegal to have the private possession of weapons or the means, such as drums, of controlling soldiers in battle. At the same time Tenmu laid the foundations for an imperial conscript army in which, theoretically, all the population were involved, owing loyalty only to him. The decree was promulgated in 684. With its emphasis upon the military arts as an essential arm of successful government, its clear hint of class distinction and its reference to mounted warriors, it contains several points which were later to be associated with the samurai class:

> In a government, military matters are the essential thing. All civil and military officials should therefore sedulously practise the use of arms and of riding on horseback. Be careful to provide an adequate supply of horses, weapons, and articles of personal costume. Those who have horses shall be made cavalry soldiers, those who have none shall be infantry soldiers. Both shall receive

Right: The élite nature of the mounted archer is shown in this painted screen, which depicts the men who were the first 'samurai' – the mounted archers of the palace guard during the Nara Period. They are wearing court robes, and have eboshi (caps) as their headgear. Each is attended by four genin (warrior attendants). Two attendants at the rear also carry bows, which may be spare ones for the horsemen.

training. Let no obstacle be thrown in the way of their assembling for this purpose.

Tenmu's reforms were continued over the next decade by his wife Jito, who succeeded him as ruler of Japan. The backbone of the conscript army was to be the infantry, levied from the general population, and linked to a central taxation system. Accurate population registers were begun, and provided the basis for a conscription system where all but the most minor use of troops (defined as the employment of a maximum of twenty soldiers) was commissioned directly by imperial authority, although this was delegated for purely practical purposes down to the governors of provinces, who were appointed by the Emperor.

The Conscript Armies

The peasants thereby conscripted became heishi (soldiers), and few men were exempt from military duties. Liability to service began at age twenty, and ended at sixty, the only exclusion being unfitness for the army or noble birth. A heishi was assigned to his local regiment, called a gundan, in which he served on ban (watch or guard) duty for certain periods each year, the rest of the time being spent on agricultural activities while the man remained on standby. Each heishi supplied his own equipment, which was carefully specified. Every soldier carried a bow and a quiver containing 50 arrows, and a pair of swords. Larger items, such as tents, were shared among groups of ten.

On the whole, the infantry were well trained and well supported, and fought as five-man squads from behind the protection of heavy wooden shields, which were as wide as a man and came up to about eye level. Very similar shields can be seen as protection for infantry in painted scrolls up to the sixteenth century, but one important piece of infantry equipment in the seventh and eighth centuries was not to survive far into samurai times. This was the ōyumi, or crossbow. The actual form of this weapon (which originated from China) is not known, as no specimen has survived in archaeological sites, and there were several possible versions of the Chinese design which could have been adopted. There appear to have been two ōyumi between each 50-man company, suggesting that they were heavy weapons operated from the ground, rather than hand arms, and another source speaks of 'arrows falling like rain', which indicates that they were variants of the Chinese repeating style of crossbow. One account of its use says that 'even tens of thousands of barbarians cannot bear up to the arrows of one machine'. But it was a complex weapon to operate, and there is considerable evidence to show that skill in

Left: Ono Harukaze, who was appointed Chinjufu-Shōgun in 878 to quell a revolt of the emishi, is seen here operating an ōyumi (crossbow).

its use gradually declined. Repeated requests were made for skilled ōyumi operators to teach the conscripts. A certain Miyoshi Kiyotsura lamented in 914 that 'those named do not yet even know of the existence of the weapon called the ōyumi, still less how to use the springs and bowstrings'. By the middle of the tenth century the ōyumi is found only as a siege weapon, and by the time the Gempei War began in 1180 it had fallen completely out of favour.

The soldiers' ban duties were supposed to be neither arduous nor long, and were theoretically organised according to a strict rota of service, but in many cases heishi would be kept on long after their allotted time, some even being made to perform agricultural work for their erstwhile commanders following a military campaign. This could cause real hardship for the men's families, and comments were made that when a man was taken for military service he was not likely to return until his hair had turned white. As a result, the absconding of peasants to avoid both taxation and military service reached serious levels by the middle of the eighth century.

The heishi's resentment at their conditions was exacerbated when more demanding military duties were required of them, because military life in Japan was not merely peacetime soldiering. In addition to ban duty every heishi was liable for guard duty in the capital, or warfare on the frontier. The former was comparatively peaceful except when rebels to the throne were involved, but the latter required military skill of the highest order. By the end of the seventh century the southwestern borders of the Yamato state were threatened only by invasion from China or Korea. This southern frontier was therefore the sea, and military duties involved garrisoning the strategic islands of Tsushima and Iki, and the mainland of Kyushu.

By contrast, the north-eastern frontier marked the division from, and almost constant warfare with, an enemy on the Japanese homeland itself. The fertile plain around what is now Tokyo, called the Kantō, bordered on to wild country. The opponents here were not rival houses of emperors or raiding foreigners, but the emishi, a tribal people of similar racial stock to the Yamato Japanese, who strongly resisted the latter's incursions into the north-east of Japan. To the Yamato rulers, the emishi were barbarians. Stockades had been established on the fringes of the area from about the middle of the seventh century, and during the eighth century a special force called the chinjufu, or Pacification Headquarters, was established in Dewa province, at the tip of northern Honshu, with the aim of extending the conquests. Here the heishi waged war when summoned, and kept watch on the emishi. This was remote country, and the rotational system involved in the conscription mechanism made such garrisoning expensive and slow to operate.

When an army was needed for a particular push against the emishi an expeditionary force would be put together from the available lists of men on standby or already on ban duties. Strategic discussions would be held at the highest levels of state, resulting in an imperial edict to fight in the name of the Emperor. An official would calculate the number of troops required, and identify the most suitable provincial gundan to be commissioned. The expeditionary force would consist of between one and three armies (gun), each of between 3,000 and 12,000 men. Command would be given to a Shōgun (general), who led his troops through a hierarchy of officers. A force of three armies would be commanded by a taishōgun (literally 'great general') who was given a ceremonial sword as the symbol of his commission. These wars, the emishi no seibatsu (the punishment of the emishi), were particularly important for the development of samurai warfare. In the words of one Japanese historian, they were 'practice for becoming bushi', the term used alternatively for samurai, meaning literally 'military gentlemen'.

The Rise of the Mounted Warrior

One of the great weaknesses of the conscript system was the reluctance of its part-time heishi to abandon their harsh, though predictable, farming lives for the uncertainty of long military expeditions. On the whole this was not a concern shared by their betters, from whose ranks the mounted officers and Shōgun would be drawn. Warrant officers were selected from those men with particular skills with 'bow and horse', a precursor of the two accomplishments which were to be so valued among samurai. The use of cavalry had long been recognised as an essential arm of an efficient fighting force, as Emperor Tenmu had personally demonstrated, and whereas the infantry crossbow was to disappear with the passing of time, the mounted archer was to go from strength to strength until as late as the fifteenth century.

As Emperor Tenmu so clearly appreciated the power of cavalry, it is not unreasonable to suppose that he would have liked to have included a state cavalry force in his conscript army. But there were problems. Horses were expensive to rear and keep, and horseback fighting was a skill that required more training than the spells of ban duty allowed. The inevitable result was to rely for cavalrymen

on those who already possessed this skill and had the resources to use it effectively. Mounted warriors, therefore, were born, not made. One source notes, significantly, that horses received as tax should be assigned 'to the care of soldiers from those regiments whose families were wealthy and able to care for the animals'. Mounted troops, therefore, were almost inevitably a minority among the armies, and quite evidently an élite. Their needs began to dominate military thinking, and within a century from Tenmu's reforms the balance was shifting from the reliance on the idealised peasant conscript army, to a philosophy expressed by an order of 788 which demanded that efforts be concentrated on men 'with cavalry skill and/or combat experience'.

Scholars disagree as to the time of the introduction of mounted warfare to Japan. Some see it as a by-product of the invaders from the continent who were to set up the Yamato state. Others identify a borrowing from the continental forces whom these settlers later engaged in warfare. By the late fifth century the Japanese were using horses on the battlefield, dressing their cavalrymen in a style of armour called keikō (hanging armour), which was the common form used throughout continental Asia. A suit of keikō consisted of numerous strips of iron or leather fastened together vertically to make a heavy suit that completely enclosed the rider's body, including his legs. Many of the haniwa (clay figurines) that have survived show warriors in keikō.

By the Nara Period (710–84), named after the first capital of Japan, mounted warriors were beginning to re-assert the traditional dominance that had been threatened by Tenmu's reforms. Warfare against the emishi was almost continuous, which placed a great strain on the loyalty of the already unwilling foot soldier. The emishi were highly skilled in light mounted warfare, a technique which came into its own when armies were attempting to pacify their territories. As long as the Yamato armies had been content to play a defensive role their crossbows and infantrymen could hold out against the emishi from within their stockades. But once the strategy changed to taking the fight to the emishi their familiarity with the territory enabled them to hit back with swift guerrilla raids. The Yamato response had to be an increased presence in two forms: infantry to garrison the territory, and cavalry to pursue and acquire new lands, with both being supplied rapidly. The conscript system proved unable to cope with these new demands, so in 792 it was officially discontinued in favour of a means of commissioning local warriors to fight on the Emperor's behalf.

Two years later, in 794, the imperial capital was transferred to Kyōto, then known as Heian-Kyō. The four centuries subsequent to the move are known as the Heian Period, and saw major developments in warfare for which the emishi had provided the initial impetus. There was also a considerable social change. It was noted earlier that the imperial call to arms had passed through the offices of the provincial governors. Appointments to such posts were made from among the court

aristocracy, and were frequently misused. On the one hand the system could produce neglect and remoteness, with offices being purchased, and absentee governorships becoming common, in a corrupt system that saw the privilege simply as a way of making money. The second way in which the system posed a threat was through an increased local identity, helped by a policy of giving such governorships to minor royals, of which there was usually a large supply. The Emperor Saga, for example, who ruled from 809 to 823, had 50 children by various concubines, and to settle such progeny in distant provinces appeared to be a sensible way of avoiding unnecessary expense at court. This process was greatly encouraged by the Fujiwara family, who frequently ruled as imperial regents,

Right: A scene from a painted scroll illustrating the story Taketori Monogatari, showing samurai on foot gathering to attack a house. They are in full yoroi armour of different coloured braid, with heavy neck guards on their helmets. (Courtesy of Christie's)

Left: The head of a haniwa (funerary statue) showing the helmet of a keiko-style armour.

Bottom right: Minamoto Yoshiie leads his army in the Later Three Years War, which lasted from 1083 until 1087. In this scroll we see excellent detail of the arms and armour of the early samurai. Note how Minamoto Yoshiie is supported by two genin (warrior attendants) carrying naginata. The one immediately to his right has pulled his head towel out from the hole in the top of his helmet to make a supportive pad, and slipped its ends under his shikoro (neck guard), the same method adopted by the leading samurai. The samurai in red has drawn his bow ready to launch an arrow from horseback. Yoshiie, as commander, wears a dragon helmet crest.

and whose daughters supplied a long succession of empresses. The excess royals were potential rivals to the Fujiwara control, and to send them away was in the Fujiwara's interests. The surnames given to these surplus princes and princesses included two in particular: Taira and Minamoto, and these two dynasties thus established were eventually to grow so strong that they challenged the imperial house itself.

The rise of such warrior houses (tsuwamono no ie) was, of course, the complete reverse of the major part of Emperor Tenmu's reforms, which had been designed to control the private use of military power. Unlike the indolent absentee landlords, the Taira and Minamoto established themselves as settled and popular lineages with strong local support, the Minamoto predominating in the north-east and the Kantō and the Taira in the south-west. The major means for attracting such local support was their military prowess. Being wealthy, the Taira and Minamoto leaders were of the very type that was now established as the military élite: the skilled mounted archer, who could take the fight to the emishi on the Emperor's behalf, with none of the inconvenience of training and transporting an army of provincial levies halfway across Japan. To add to the continuing threat from the emishi, there were robber gangs to be dealt with, and pirate raids, and the occasional rebellion, often fomented by a dissatisfied former courtier.

It must not be thought that by abandoning the imperial conscript system the central Heian government was abandoning its responsibilities to govern. Instead, prompted by a realisation that the system was inefficient – and too heavily reliant on infantry rather than the more useful cavalry – the emperors had simply privatised the service, and commissioned military activities from those on whom it could rely. The providers of such services were those who combined a respectable aristocratic lineage with proven skills in mounted warfare. There was a danger in such a policy, but it is a danger seen more clearly with the benefit of hindsight. By the end of the twelfth century one of these aristocratic clans would indeed have supplanted the imperial power, but viewed from the standpoint of earlier centuries the commissioning of military activities from what were in effect upper-class mercenary soldiers was a sensible alternative to the clumsy apparatus of the discredited conscription system. The passage of time over the next three hundred years only served to confirm this view. If a rebel to the throne should arise, his incursion was never seen as evidence that the scheme was not working because there was always a loyal landowner somewhere in the vicinity who could be relied upon to accept the imperial commission to chastise him. Any competition that existed between the rival clans was not usually expressed through civil war, but in a desire to show that their family were the best to be granted further commissions, and the evidence for this only came through the successive performance of good service rendered in the Emperor's name.

An example of the government's firm control of the situation is illustrated by the service rendered by Minamoto Yoshiie in the 'Later Three Years War' of 1083–7. The results of Yoshiie's expedition were in the state's best interests, but because Yoshiie had conducted it without receiving the appropriate imperial commission the government refused to reward him, and stuck to its guns even when the furious Yoshiie threw the severed heads of the rebels into a ditch. Although sometimes interpreted as an act of weakness by the government, its strict insistence on not recognising a private act of warfare as its own unless properly commissioned shows the control the centralised state was exerting even at this late stage. The purchaser/provider model of military control was therefore handled through a policy that was ready to adapt to changing circumstances, yet maintained its own authority every bit as strictly as Tenmu had policed his conscript army.

The First Samurai

It was noted earlier that military service involved guard duty in the capital as well as service on the frontiers, and it is from this other form of muster that the word 'samurai' arose. It comes from the classical Japanese verb saburau (to serve), its noun-derivative being saburai or samurai. The earliest use of the term appears to date from the eighth century, but has no military context, and refers simply to domestic servants who had the care of elderly people. The notion of service gradually came to encompass a military dimension, and by the tenth century we read of provincial warriors going to the capital to

Right: The death of Taira Masakado. The Shōmonki, which chronicles Masakado's exploits, is the first of the gunkimono, which provide a valuable record of samurai warfare both in its ideal and its reality.

serve as 'samurai', a role which involved guard duty on behalf of the imperial line or the Fujiwara regents. They were organised in contingents called samurai-dokoro (samurai units). Minamoto Mitsunaka (912–97) (the son of Tsunemoto, who was the first to bear the surname of Minamoto), was among the earliest of that illustrious clan to act as a samurai, and was commissioned by the Fujiwara. In time this specific role of guard service in the capital merged with the wider concept of warrior behaviour to provide the notion of samurai as it is understood today.

Successive generations of Minamoto and Taira developed the tradition of samurai service, quelling rebels on the emperor's behalf, pushing back the frontiers of imperial territory, and growing rich on the proceeds of both. The beginnings of the use of the term samurai coincide with the emergence of the gunkimono (war stories), which are the most important sources for how these warriors looked and behaved. The earliest of such chronicles is the Shōmonki, which describes

17

Left: This scroll, showing samurai and their attendants in camp before a battle, reminds us of the social distinction between warriors. They are sitting before a maku (curtain). All are wearing eboshi (caps), but the attendants have simple dō-maru armour and carry naginata, except one who has a simple helmet with a neck guard of mail. Others, presumably grooms, tend the horses, and one has a drum on his back. By contrast, the samurai in the bottom right corner has a yoroi armour and carries a bow. (Courtesy of Christie's)

the revolt of Taira Masakado. As well as introducing us to the appearance and activities of the samurai, Shōmonki illustrates the points made above of the commissioning process for the subjugation of rebels, descriptions developed in the later Konjaku Monogatari, which begins with Taira Masakado's revolt.

As his name implies, Masakado was of the Taira clan which by the tenth century had split into several branches. In his youth Masakado served as 'samurai' to the imperial regent Fujiwara Tadahira, but returned later to the Kantō where he became engaged in warfare with rivals. This developed into open rebellion in 939 when he attacked and captured the headquarters of the governor of Hitachi province. Masakado attempted to justify his actions by reference to the grasping nature of the governor's rule, which may well have been true, but he then went on to conquer the provinces of Kōzuke and Shimotsuke, and proclaimed himself as the new Emperor of the Kantō. The commissioning system moved into action, and Masakado was killed the following year by his cousin Taira Sadamori and Fujiwara Hidesato. His head was sent to the capital as proof of work completed.

The descriptions in the Shōmonki and the Konjaku Monogatari provide an early glimpse of samurai warfare. The armies consist of combinations of mounted archers and peasant infantry, and, like Tenmu's conscript armies, are disbanded once a campaign is over. The difference between the two situations is that Taira Masakado's army involves an established personal tie of loy-

TOKUGAWA IEYASU AT THE PROVISIONING OF ODAKA, 1560
Tokugawa Ieyasu (1542–1616), who re-established the position of Shōgun in 1603, was one of the most outstanding practitioners of samurai warfare. This plate shows an incident in his early career when he was still a vassal of Imagawa Yoshimoto, and consequently in arms against Oda Nobunaga. Odaka, one of the Imagawa fortresses, was hard-pressed and in need of supplies. Tokugawa Ieyasu launched a diversionary raid against a nearby fort, causing the Oda army to withdraw a sizeable proportion of their men from Odaka. Ieyasu thereupon led a pack horse unit into Odaka under the noses of the weakened besiegers.

Ieyasu is shown wearing the armour preserved in the Kunozan Tōshōgū Shrine Museum in Shizuoka which he is believed to have worn during this incident. Attributions of certain armours to certain famous figures are often very difficult to verify. In some cases a samurai's descendants would have a suit of armour made for their late lord's departed spirit. Stylistically, I would have dated this armour later than 1560, but the Kunozan Museum firmly associate it with Ieyasu then. It is a magnificent example of the samurai 'battledress', simple and practical in design, yet made stunning in appearance by the use of gold lacquer in place of the customary black or brown. The rounded helmet is a zunari-kabuto, a style easy to produce and which became very common on Japanese battlefields. Behind him fly the flags of Honda Tadakatsu and Sakai Tadatsugu, two men who were to fight beside him for the whole of their adult lives. The pack horse leaders are the lowest ranks of ashigaru (foot soldiers). They wear no armour except a simple jingasa (war hat), which bears the mon of the Tokugawa. The wooden castle tower and gateway, typical of the period, are based on data recently made available from the excavations of the site of Sakurai castle, part of which has been reconstructed.

alty rather than impressed service. As the experience against the emishi had shown, such links made it easier and quicker to raise an army. It is this absence of a standing army which explains the widely fluctuating numbers which Masakado leads. The need to assemble such a force is also cited as one reason for his final defeat, because only 400 men were with him by the time his enemies attacked. The word 'samurai' is not used as a description of warriors in the Shōmonki. Instead we read tsuwamono (warrior), and there is one brief reference to a concept called tsuwamono no michi (the way of the warrior), a distant precursor of the better known bushidō. The term used in the later chronicle Konjaku Monogatari, which also describes Masakado's rebellion, is kyūba no michi (the way of horse and bow), where the context implies that the certain élite status enjoyed by these fine mounted archers depended as much on their ancestry as on their martial prowess. A story in the Konjaku Monogatari contains the following grudging praise in its description of the warrior Settsu no Zenji Yasumasa: 'Although he was not of a warrior house, he was not in the least degree inferior to such a warrior.' It is interesting to note that the comment is not referring to any ignoble ancestry on Yasumasa's part. He had in fact occupied the posts of governor of four provinces, and was a household official of the Fujiwara. The problem was that his pedigree was not that of the new élite of warrior houses for whom the Konjaku Monogatari was compiled.

Early Samurai Battles

The élite nature of the samurai is a very important factor to remember when using the accounts of the period to study samurai warfare, because they were written for an aristocratic public who wished to read of the deeds of their own class, and preferably their own family's ancestors. For this reason the gunkimono have to be treated with some reservation as a historical record, and must be set against the more sober accounts recorded in court diaries or official chronicles. For example, the foot soldiers who accompanied the samurai are frequently ignored, but the Shōmonki is an exception in that it states that Masakado's armies contain a large number of foot soldiers, who fight from behind walls of shields, just as in the earlier conscript armies.

Seeing the state of Masakado's troops, the enemy formed a wall of shields and moved out to deliver the decisive blow. But before the rival forces were upon them, Masakado dispatched his foot soldiers, launching a counter-attack that all but brought the fighting to an end ... Yoshikane was panic-stricken and fled with his men, all of them dragging their shields as they went.

Elsewhere we read of soldiers 'slinging their shields on their backs'. In its description of Masakado's final battle the chronicle notes the blowing of a gale, which blew down Masakado's shield wall, and 'because of this both sides put aside their shields and did battle without them'. Barriers of shields are also mentioned in descriptions of an exchange of arrow fire before the start of a battle, a tactic which was to become de rigueur for a samurai encounter.

They turned towards their sacred battle standard, waved a banner, and struck a drum when Masakado's army came to view on the distant horizon ... Fortunately the direction of the wind was in Masakado's favour, and his arrows flew through the air, unerringly hitting their target.

Many of the warriors who fought on foot would not have been simple peasants, but would have been acting in the capacity of warriors' attendants (genin or shojū), who had particular responsibilities towards their masters. The duties included the grooming and feeding of the horse, carrying equipment, and the gathering of heads of enemies killed in battle. When one of Masakado's enemies attempts to enlist one of Masakado's followers as a traitor, he promises him promotion 'to mounted retainer'. In painted scrolls the attendant usually appears in a simpler form of armour than that of the samurai, and he is often bare-legged. He may wear an eboshi (cap) rather than a helmet, and his weapon is frequently the curved-bladed naginata. Even though their primary duties were those of servants to the individual samurai, they did take part in fighting, as painted scrolls such as the Heiji Monogatari Emaki attest. Such figures as are available suggest an equal number of attendants to samurai. Thus the Konjaku Monogatari

Above: The use of the kumade (rake), in bringing down a samurai, who is carrying a naginata. This illustration depicts an incident during the sixteenth century, but such techniques changed little throughout samurai history.

describes a force of 70 mounted to 30 foot, while two other sources mention bands of 15 or 16 horsemen accompanied by 20 or more infantry, and seven or eight horsemen with ten or more foot. In the later chronicle Heiji Monogatari there is an honourable mention for a certain warrior's attendant called Jirō, who pulled a rival from his horse by bringing his kumade (rake) down on to the horseman's helmet. The victim would have become a trophy for Jirō's master had he not cut through the shaft of the kumade with his sword, and made his escape. The other foot soldiers present at battles, impressed into service by the landowner, carried out exploits that remain largely unrecorded in the gunkimono. Nevertheless, in considerations of samurai warfare, it is important to recognise both their presence and their usefulness, and not to assume that all fighting was carried out from the back of a horse.

In summary, it can be seen that the formation of the samurai class and the development of samurai warfare involved two major factors. The first was technological development through the use of horses, armour and bows, and the second was the social aspect of the establishment of 'warrior houses', who were able to exploit the means of warfare. The Shōmonki and Konjaku Monogatari accounts both show that these factors were slowly being formulated. At this time the war bands still consist of part-time warriors, who would otherwise manage their agricultural lands, on which worked the attendants and the peasants who still made up a major part of their armies. These armies were rapidly recruited and readily disbanded. The following chapter will illustrate how these factors were further developed when samurai fought samurai in the fierce battles of the Gempei War.

Chapter 2
MILITARY GENTLEMEN

The Way of Horse and Bow

The mounted archers of the Heian Period provide the first of a series of popular images of samurai warfare to be encountered through Japanese history. In this chapter we shall take a critical look at the reality behind these images, using the available evidence to evaluate the bushi, the 'military gentlemen'.

We begin with the samurai's appearance. The standard 'samurai armour' of the Heian period had now evolved from the earlier lamellar keikō into the version familiar from contemporary illustrations, and was known as the yoroi (harness), or ōyoroi (great harness), which weighed about 30 kilograms. The body of the armour, the dō, was divided into four parts, giving the yoroi its characteristic box-like appearance. Two large shoulder plates, the sode, were worn, fastened at the rear of the armour by a large ornamental bow called the agemaki. The agemaki allowed the arms free movement while keeping the body always covered. Two guards were attached to the shoulder-straps to prevent the tying cords from being cut, and a sheet of ornamented leather was fastened across the front to prevent the bow string catching on any projection. The helmet bowl was commonly of 8–12 plates, fastened together with large projecting conical rivets, and the neck was protected with a heavy five-piece neck guard called a shikoro, which hung from the bowl. The top four plates were folded back at the front to form the fukigayeshi, which stopped downward cuts aimed at the horizontal lacing of the shikoro. Normally the eboshi (cap) was worn under the helmet, but if the samurai's hair were very long the motodori (pigtail) was allowed to pass through the tehen, the hole in the centre of the helmet's crown, where the plates met. As an alternative to the eboshi a towel could be tied round the head as a pad, the ends being brought out of the tehen and tucked under between the bowl and the shikoro. No armour was worn on the right arm, so as to leave it free for drawing the bow, but a simple armour sleeve with sewn-on plates was worn on the left arm.

The immense detail of appearance and activity of the bushi recorded in the gunki-mono does not extend to long discussions of tactics. The overall aim in fighting battles at this time is nearly always the straightforward destruction of an opponent, yet, once achieved, the rewards to the victor are somewhat obscure. Reward in the form of the acquisition of the victim's lands could only come about as a grant from the officials who had commissioned the campaign in the first place. If the opponent were a rebel it was more than likely that some proportion of his forfeited lands would be given to the victor, but the samurai appear to have respected the rules, unlike their descendants in the sixteenth century, where the rapid seizure of one's defeated enemy's lands was the only means of acquiring new territory.

The Archery Duel

Politics aside, the gunkimono tell of a style of battle which is put forward as the samurai ideal, where the warrior's spirit and prowess may be shown to the best advantage, and in spite of some omissions, the gunkimono do correct some popular misconceptions about the samurai. For example, in contrast to the common image of the samurai today, there are only two references in the entire Shōmonki chronicle to the use of the sword, because the weapon par excellence of the warrior was the bow, fired from horseback. The use of bows and arrows is the most commonly described military activity in the gunkimono.

The use of the bow in Japan has a long history. There is evidence of its use for hunting in the Jōmon Period (c.700–250 BC), and it was used in war during the Yayoi Period (400 BC–AD 300). The design of the traditional Japanese bow which the samurai wielded is still used today in the martial art of kyūdo. It was about 2.5 metres long, and constructed from laminations of deciduous wood and bamboo, reinforced with rattan. The whole bow was then lacquered. Because of its use from the saddle of a horse it was fired from

Right: Excellent detail of samurai armour as seen from the rear is shown in this print by Yoshitoshi, depicting Minamoto Yoshiie accompanied by a genin. His armour is a multicoloured dō-maru, its constituent parts held together by the agemaki bow tied at the rear, but without sode (shoulder guards). His scabbard is covered with tiger skin, and a bow string reel hangs from it. His quiver is protected by a cloth cover. He wears an eboshi (cap) on his head. This slide was kindly supplied by Rolf Degener (Japanese Prints) of Düsseldorf.

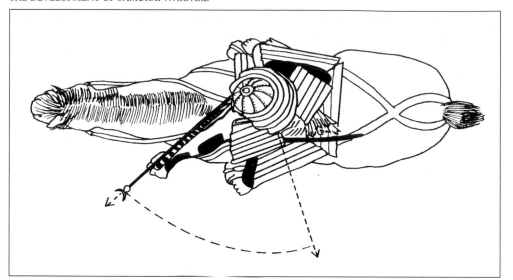

Left: Diagram showing the effective angle of fire available to a mounted archer wearing a yoroi, which was almost always restricted to the left side of the horse.

about a third of the way up its length. Arrows were made of bamboo and were carried in box-shaped quivers called ebira, the shafts of the arrows being tied by a cord. The archer would lift an individual arrow clear, then pull it down and fit it to his bow.

The impression given by many of the gunkimono accounts is that battles began with an exchange of arrows, followed by a number of individual combats, after which the fight became general. The first arrows fired in battle would often be the kabura-ya, arrows with large perforated wooden heads in the shape of a turnip, which hummed as they flew through the air. The sound was a call to the gods to draw their attention to the great deeds of bravery which were about to be performed by rival warriors. This had a great symbolic value, but then the samurai would commence a fierce archery exchange where the arrow heads were of pointed steel.

The Konjaku Monogatari includes one very detailed account of a set-piece battle which involves an arrow duel (ya-awase). The encounter is fought between the rivals Minamoto Mitsuru and Taira Yoshifumi, who agree to settle their differences in a pre-arranged set-piece battle. A suitable date and time is agreed, and each turns up accompanied by a force of between 500 and 600 men. The armies are separated by about 100 metres. After an exchange of messengers confirming the commanders' intentions to do battle, both sides begin to shoot arrows, but as the two armies approach Yoshifumi sends word to Mitsuru that they should fight a single combat. The challenge

is accepted, and the two samurai fight a duel by shooting at each other from galloping horses, a technique similar to the martial art of yabusame still seen at festivals in Japan, where mounted horsemen discharge arrows at targets.

> Then fitting arrows with forked heads to their bows, they urged their horses toward each other, and each let off his first arrow at the other. Intending that his next arrow would hit his rival without fail, each drew his bow and released the arrow as he galloped past. Then they drew up their horses and turned ...

After three arrows both consider that honour is satisfied, and the armies withdraw.

Mounted archery while wearing ōyoroi must have been much more difficult than present-day yabusame, regardless of the fact that the target was not only moving, but also trying to kill you at the same time. The archer could only shoot to his left side, along an arc of about 45 degrees from about 'nine o'clock to eleven o'clock' relative to the direction of movement. The horse's neck prevented any closer angle firing. Certain accounts imply that it was the power of an archer's shot, rather than its accuracy, which most impressed commentators. Minamoto Yoshiie was credited with firing an arrow through three suits of armour hung from the branch of a tree.

The preliminary duel of arrows enabled the samurai to exercise 'the way of horse and bow' in the manner for which they had been trained. Large numbers of casualties are likely to have been rare, and there is an unusual account of an archery duel and a series of challenges before the Battle of Kurikara in 1183, which was carried out for a very subtle purpose. Minamoto Yoshinaka planned to divide his forces and surround the Taira army, but needed to cover these movements and hold the Taira in position. His solution was to conceal his manoeuvres by fighting a prolonged arrow duel.

Most encounters, of course, did not allow such niceties of behaviour to take place. Many start with surprise attacks, catching the opponent off guard in an ambush or a night raid, but an archery duel is usually included. A notable example is the archer Minamoto Tametomo, who fought during the attack on the Shirakawa-den in the Hōgen Incident in 1156 and shot many arrows clean through saddles, horses and his opponents, as the Hōgen Monogatari tells us:

> The arrow pierced the breastplate of Itō Roku, who was first in the enemy's van, and passed through him, turned the sleeve of Itō Go's armour inside out and hung there. Itō Roku at once fell dead from his horse.

Later in the same action we read:

> Tametomo shot before him and his arrow whistled through the air. It pierced the pommel of Yamada's saddle, and cutting through the skirt of his armour and his own body too, went through the cantle and stuck out three inches beyond. For a moment he seemed to be held in the saddle by the arrow, but suddenly he fell head-first to the ground.

Minamoto Tametomo is also credited with using a bow and arrow to sink a ship. The massive arrowhead struck the overladen boat just above the waterline and split the planking, allowing in enough water to capsize the vessel. The hero of the Minamoto, Nasu no Yoichi, is another famous example of sharpshooting. At the Battle of Yashima in 1184 the Taira hung a fan from the mast of one of their ships and invited the Minamoto to shoot it down, hoping thereby to persuade them to waste precious arrows. Nasu no Yoichi hit the fan with his first arrow, even though he was on horseback in the water and

the boat he was aiming at was bobbing up and down. Such a dramatic response to their challenge greatly demoralised the Taira, and helped in their defeat.

Not all archery was conducted from horseback. Samurai would also shoot on foot from behind the protection of the foot soldiers' wooden shields, as shown by the Azuma Kagami account of the Shōkyū War of 1221:

> ... thirty court warriors made a stand, raining arrows on the Easterners from behind their shields ... As Hatano Gorō Yoshishige stepped out, he was hit in the right eye. His senses reeled, but he was able to shoot an answering arrow.

Single Combat and the Samurai Sword

Following the archery duel, one or more feats of individual combat would take place. The word used in the gunkimono for single combat between samurai is ikki-uchi (single mounted warrior) fighting, which was to become the norm for worthy opponents. Such a contest would traditionally begin with one warrior calling out a challenge, in which he would recount at length his elaborate and honourable pedigree. This is so common in the gunkimono that it must have some basis in fact, but it is hard to see how a samurai could have much leisure for such a challenge once battle was given. The challenge would be answered from within the opposing army, thus providing a recognised mechanism whereby only worthy opponents would meet in combat. The Hōgen Monogatari, which describes events of 1156, contains an excellent example, which also shows the importance attached to being the first into battle, and how the deeds of one's ancestors could make up for one's own lack of battle experience:

> I am not such a great man as men go, but I am an inhabitant of Iga province, a follower of the Lord of Aki, and 28 years old. My name is Yamada Kosaburō Koreyuki. I am the grandson of Yamada no Shōji Yukisue, who was well known among the aristocracy for being the first to go into battle under the Lord of Bizen at the attack on Yoshihito, Lord of Tsushima. My grandfather also captured innumerable mountain robbers and highwaymen. I too have been many times in battle and made a name for myself.

英雄三十六歌撰

さざなみや
しがのみやこは
あれにしを
むかしながらの
山ざくら哉

平忠度

Left: Taira Tadanori (1144-84), who was killed at the Battle of Ichi-no-tani, is the subject of this print, which offers a clear description of samurai armour as viewed from the front. Over an elaborate yoroi-hitatare (armour robe), embroidered with pom-poms, Tadanori wears a multicoloured braid ōyoroi armour. He wears a nodowa (throat guard) and the details of his ebira (quiver) are clearly shown. He has fur-covered boots, and wears the left kote (sleeve) only. His right arm would be left free for drawing the bow. Behind him walks an attendant, who wears a simple dō-maru and carries a naginata.

Right: In this vivid scroll painting Nasu Yoichi Munetaka begs to be allowed to try his skill at shooting a fan from the mast of a Taira ship at the Battle of Yashima in 1184. His leader, Minamoto Yoshit-sune, is depicted wearing a horō on the back of his armour. The wooden shields are well-represented, including the supporting struts behind them. (Courtesy of Christie's)

The need of the individual samurai was for glory and recognition, and on the whole the most glorious and chivalric of samurai activities are confined to acts of individual combat. An individual combat using bows was noted above, but it was more likely to be fought using edged weapons. When close combat began the bow would be handed to a warrior attendant and cutting weapons would be used, the best known of these being the celebrated 'samurai sword', which in those days was a tachi, a style of sword carried with the cutting edge downwards, slung at the side of the armour from a strong belt.

Kumagai and Hirayama both bore themselves most valiantly, one charging forward when the other gave back, and neither yielding to the other in strength and boldness, hewing at the foe with loud shouts while the sparks flew from their weapons.

A sword is used in a swift opportunistic stroke following the archery duel at the Battle of Shinohara (1183):

> Nyūzen, who was famous for the rapidity of his movements, catching him off guard, suddenly drew his sword and aimed a lightning thrust under his helmet.

In the later Shōkyūki, which deals with ex-Emperor Go-Toba's rebellion of 1221, we read of a warrior's attendant using a kumade (the polearm with several hooks at the end) to unbalance an opponent so that his master's sword may be used in a similar way:

> ... he rushed up and hooked his grapnel into the crown of Satsuma's helmet, pulled him close, and struck off his head.

It is usually accepted that the Japanese sword developed as a fairly long, curved-bladed weapon to that it could more easily be wielded from the saddle, but there are so few accounts of sword combat while mounted that this idea is difficult to support. One might speculate that the reason for the ikki-uchi style of combat was largely determined by the samurai's primary role as a mounted archer. While mounted and wearing a suit of armour built like a rigid box, he was effectively a mobile and well-protected 'gun platform'. When unable to wield his bow he was comparatively ungainly and unwieldy, able only to grapple in the most clumsy fashion from horseback. His protective costume, while not unduly heavy, was not designed to allow him to take the fight to the enemy, and was certainly not helpful in allowing a sword to be used from the saddle. However, if there were time to dismount successfully from a fallen horse, some excellent swordplay could be seen from samurai whose desire to survive overcame any disadvantages posed by the weight or design of their armour. At the Battle of Shinohara:

> Arikuni, having penetrated very deeply into the ranks of the foe, had his horse

But, as was implied by the phrase kyūba no michi, a samurai's worth was measured in terms of his prowess with the bow, rather than the sword.

To the modern mind the concept of the samurai and his sword are almost inseparable. The sword has acquired a quasi-religious – almost mystical – symbolism and is wielded in a way that often appears to be a combination of superhuman skill and technological perfection. But at this time the traditions to be associated with the Japanese sword were just developing, as were the techniques of sword fighting. There is only one incident in Heike Monogatari which implies sword combat while still mounted, when two comrades support each other as they lead an assault on the Taira fortress of Ichi-no-tani in 1184:

Left: The attack on the fortress of Ichi-no-tani during the Gempei War, from a woodblock-printed edition of the Gempei Seisuki. The arms and armour of samurai of the period are clearly illustrated.

shot from under him, and then while he was fighting on foot, his helmet was struck from his head, so that he looked like a youth fighting, with his long hair streaming in all directions. By this time his arrows were exhausted, so he drew his sword and laid about him mightily, until, pierced by seven or eight shafts, he met his death still on his feet and glaring at his enemies.

There is a similar description of Kajiwara Genda's desperate fight at Ichi-no-tani (1184), and during the fight at Mizushima (1183), fought aboard ship and thus unencumbered by horses, we also see some swordplay:

And so shouting their war cry, they began the fight, drawing their bows and pouring in a hail of arrows until they came to close quarters, when they drew their swords and engaged each other hand to hand.

Single Combat and the Dagger
Several examples of sword fighting are recorded in Heike Monogatari, but the impression one gets in reading contemporary accounts of individual combat is that the tantō (dagger) was much more important than the sword in deciding the outcome of a

one-to-one contest. An example is the account in Heike Monogatari of the fight that eventually led to the death of Taira Tadanori:

But Satsuma-no-kami, who had been brought up at Kumano, was famous for his strength, and was extremely active and agile besides, so clutching Tadazumi he pulled him from his horse, dealing him two stabs with his tantō while he was yet in the saddle, and following them with another as he was falling. The first two blows fell on his armour and failed to pierce it, while the third wounded him in the face but was not mortal ...

During the same battle, which was Ichi-no-tani (1184), the single combat between Etchū Zenji Moritoshi and Inomata Noritsuna began with unarmed techniques, and ended with a tantō.

Inomata immediately leapt upon him, snatched his tantō from his side, and pulling up the skirt of his armour, stabbed him so deeply thrice that the hilt and fist went in after the blade. Having thus dispatched him he cut off his head ...

The following account from the Shōkyūki describes the full process of an archery duel

Rokurō's helmet down as far as the shoulder-straps of his armour. Rokurō looked to be in danger, but just at that moment Takeda Hachirō came upon the scene, and pushing Rokurō aside, cut off his assailant's head.

The Samurai in Group Combat

Apart from recounting noble individual deeds of archery duels, challenges and single combat, the gunkimono also contain many accounts which show how unheroic much of samurai warfare could be. Many battles were carried out by surprise attacks. These could involve night raids on buildings, setting them on fire, and indiscriminately slaughtering all who ran out: men, women and children alike. Most of the battles described have some element of surprise built in, just to give one side an advantage. In such cases the ends were regarded as justifying the means. Minamoto Tametomo is quoted as saying:

> According to my experience, there is nothing so advantageous in striking down enemies as a night attack ... If we set fire to three sides and secure the fourth, those fleeing the flames will be struck down by arrows, and for those who seek to avoid the arrows, there will be no escape from the flames.

There were no doubt good military reasons for such an approach. When two armies engaged both were likely to be similarly equipped, and to catch an opponent off guard could be the only way of achieving any relative superiority. A graphic account of such an operation occurs in the account of the Shōkyū War of 1221 in the chronicle Azuma Kagami:

> At lamp-lighting time the houses of the court warriors were all set on fire. As the flames spread, bringing destruction in their wake, the despairing and bewildered townsfolk ran wildly in all directions, afraid to live and afraid to die ... Eastern warriors filled the neighbouring provinces, seeking out foot soldiers who had fled the battlefields. Heads rolled constantly; naked blades were wiped over and over. Even on foot, it was scarcely possible to thread a way

Above: The single combat between Etchū Zenji Moritoshi and Inomata Noritsuna at the Battle of Ichi-no-tani in 1184, from a woodblock printed edition of Heike Monogatari.

in 1221, which is concluded by a fight using tantō:

Pulling an outer arrow from his quiver and fitting it to his rattan-striped bow, he drew the shaft to its full length and let fly. The arrow pierced the breast plate of Takeda Rokurō's chief retainer, who was standing at the left side of his lord, and shot through to the clover-leaf bow (the agemaki) at the armour's back, toppling the retainer instantly from his horse. Saburō shot again, and his second arrow passed completely through the neck bone of one of Takeda Rokurō's pages. Then Rokurō and Saburō grappled together and fell from their horses. As they tumbled back and forth, Saburō drew his dagger and pulled the crown of

Left: The most deadly weapon in the repertoire of samurai warfare was fire. It contradicted the ideal of samurai behaviour, but was frequently used, as in this example which is of the burning of the fortress of Ichi-no-tani during the Gempei War, from a woodblock-printed edition of the Gempei Seisuki.

through the bodies of men and horses clogging the intersections.

Such accounts imply a huge discrepancy between ideal and reality in samurai warfare. However, it is important to note that these two different types of description actually occur side by side in the same story, with no implication that one is less moral than the other. The only way in which the samurai could be regarded as fighting in two different and contradictory ways lies in the very real conflict between individual glory and the needs of the group.

The notion of group loyalty in samurai warfare is as closely tied to their élite nature as is single combat and the seeking of a worthy opponent. Whereas the accounts of actual fighting in the gunkimono dwell heavily on single combat, the élite nature of samurai warfare did not depend solely on choosing a worthy opponent for one's individual skills. The samurai had to be a leader, and the samurai general had to be the leader of armies. His strategic skills in choosing ground, and the logistics of supply and recruitment, were all important to his success. But once battle had been joined, and the archery duel was over, the fight became general, with a multitude of individual or group combats taking place. In these situations the samurai tended to fight their own battles with little reference to their commander. The commander, for his part, would not have been sitting at the rear controlling troops, surrounded by a huge bodyguard, as his

descendants were to do, but would be in the thick of the fighting himself. His orders would have been given, and from that point on little overall control was retained, as he, too, sought a worthy opponent. The tenuous nature of the organisation within the army also mitigated against chess-board precision. Samurai fought as units of individuals, whose reputations would be enhanced only by personal prowess. More importantly, perhaps, individual reputations would not necessarily suffer by the defeat of the army in which the valiant samurai had acquitted himself so well.

Thus samurai warfare of the Heian Period does not give the impression of being carried out by disciplined and drilled armies. This fails to convey the whole truth, however, because there was a great deal of discipline and organisation, but this was to be found in units smaller than the overall army. The limits of such organisation were probably small groups on the battlefield of twenty or so warriors who supported one another, linked by family or other ties. Their companions would have been relatives or comrades with whom they had trained and had fought previously side by side. Such a group would have been able to co-ordinate their movements among the overall chaos of a samurai battle. While one of their number fought his worthy opponent, the others provided support. The close co-operation between the Minamoto relatives during the night attack described earlier is an example of this being used successfully. Of the 'glue' which held

Right: This is a scroll painting showing the burning of a defended building by samurai. As noted in the text, this was a favourite means of attack. A group of samurai are galloping away, accompanied by their attendants who run along beside them. (Courtesy of Christie's)

these groups together, family ties were the strongest, followed by long-standing lord/vassal relationships.

The organisation within the successful army, therefore, would consist of a hierarchy of vertical relationships, family, vassal or both, linked horizontally by other ties of marriage, agreed responsibility, or obligation. An example of the latter would be a debt of honour to a warrior who had saved another's life. Among the weakest ties of all were alliances between clans, which were particularly prone to break once battle had been joined, and a half-hearted alliance quickly became treason. The large-scale battles of the sixteenth century contain several examples of this, but such activities are less common in the smaller wars of the Gempei Period. Other comparatively weak social ties were caused by the recruitment of peasant warriors, virtually by press-gang, who were poorly equipped and so carelessly registered that any desertion was untraceable. The Taira army that pursued Minamoto Yoshinaka in 1183 lost much of its strength from

peasant desertion before it even came in sight of the enemy.

To summarise, therefore: samurai warfare in the Heian Period consisted of two major types of battlefield activity: ikki-uchi (single combat), or group combat. The first type has been adequately described above. The second is that of the general fight on the battlefield, into which attendants and lowly peasants would be drawn, though in all the accounts of the period the impression is given that it is the fighting of samurai against samurai that constitutes the totality of samurai warfare. Within this second form may be identified a certain co-ordination between small groups committed to the overall battle plan, but with a prime loyalty to one another, in an organisational system which did not stifle the demands of individual glory. Samurai warfare, therefore, worked to two potentially competing agendas: the individual and the group, and the mark of the successful commander during the Heian Period was the ability to balance the two, to his own, and to his followers' mutual advantage.

Chapter 3
THE WARRIOR MONKS

The Sōhei of Kyōto and Nara

The history of samurai warfare has so far been told from the viewpoint of warring families, or between those loyal to the Emperor and rebels to the throne. Yet throughout much of the time of civil war there was often a third force in Japanese military politics: the armies linked to religious institutions. In the early years these armies were the fierce sōhei (monk soldiers or 'warrior monks') of the major Buddhist temples of Kyōto and Nara. Later in history their place was taken by the more populist peasant armies, whose fanaticism was fuelled by their religious affiliation to sects such as the Ikkō-ikki. This chapter will examine the first of these phenomena, asking to what extent the warrior monks constituted a real threat to samurai hegemony in the early wars.

The sōhei are among the most romantic figures in the history of samurai warfare. The first warrior monks had their origins in the rapid growth to power of the major Buddhist institutions in central Japan, which were located around the capital city of Kyōto and the former capital of Nara, which lies about 50 kilometres to the south. Nara was the first permanent capital of Japan, and Buddhism was a very important influence on the lives of the courtiers. Its main temples, the Kōfuku-ji and the Tōdai-ji, were richly endowed. Buddhism at Nara thus grew to exercise considerable political influence, and it was partly to escape this that the capital was moved to Heian (Kyōto) in 894. Kyōto's location had been deliberately chosen because, according to the laws of Chinese geomancy, the north-east was the direction from which evil could strike, and the Kyōto site was protected from this quarter by a complex of Buddhist monasteries built on the mountain called Mount Hiei. They had been

Below: Mount Hiei, location of the warrior monk temple of Enryaku-ji, as seen from its daughter temple Miidera, near the shore of Lake Biwa.

founded by the monk Saichō (767–862) who is known by the posthumous name of Dengyō Daishi. At its height the Mount Hiei complex consisted of more than 3,000 religious buildings, including the major temple called the Enryaku-ji. Miidera, located at the foot of Mount Hiei, was Enryaku-ji's daughter temple. There had been immediate jealousy from the older foundations of Nara when Mount Hiei was established, as they saw their historic pre-eminence threatened by these new institutions. Their suspicions were well-founded because the religious power of Mount Hiei came to exert a formidable influence on the inhabitants of the new capital.

All these great monastic centres were associated with the Tendai sect of Japanese Buddhism, so the rivalry that developed between them was not about religious doctrine as

such, but had to do with wealth and prestige. It was not long before the temples began arming themselves and training their inmates as soldiers. The earliest records of rivalry are between factions of monks within the same area, when disputes arose in 968 at Nara and 981 on Mount Hiei, over the choice of new abbots. In that same year of 981 we also read of the first demonstration by warrior monks in the streets of Kyōto. Frustrated in their efforts to have certain requests satisfied by the government, they marched through the capital in an armed demonstration to place their demands before a terrified Court. The act was to be repeated on several occasions, and for the next hundred years their incursions alarmed the superstitious courtiers and frightened the ordinary citizens of Kyōto.

It is possible to conclude from the recorded reactions of civilians that by the time of the Gempei War the warrior monks constituted the most formidable standing army in central Japan. It is questionable, however, whether those who suffered their violence were more frightened by the monks themselves or the spiritual power they represented. The monks must in any case have been an intimidating sight, for the sōhei represented in scroll paintings or later woodblock printed books always look very rough characters. When on demonstrations they are dressed in full monastic robes of black, white, purple or saffron. Their shaven heads bear a few days' growth of bristles, and headbands are tied across their sweaty foreheads. Other illustrations depicting battles between monastic armies and samurai show monks wearing the traditional cowl over suits of armour, which were usually a simple wrap-around dō-maru, or the more elaborate yoroi with a breastplate. Fuller head protection would of course necessitate the wearing of a helmet, and in the battle between warrior monks of Nara and the Taira family depicted in the Kasuga Gongen scroll, we see a monk army that is fully armoured and thus appears almost indistinguishable from ordinary samurai.

Monk weapons included the usual sword and dagger as worn by samurai, and bows and arrows. There is often the addition of the monk's traditional polearm weapon called a naginata, which was a form of glaive. The blade was similar to a sword blade, but often much wider, and was fixed on a polearm

Below: A typical sōhei, with shaven head, uproots a tree in a characteristically belligerent mood.

Left: Warrior monks, variously armoured and attired, carry the sacred omikoshi of Sannō down to Kyōto.

handle between three and seven feet long. In the eleventh and twelfth centuries the form called the shobuzukuri naginata was preferred, which had a somewhat shorter handle and a huge blade. Slashing strokes were the usual way of fighting, and could produce very nasty wounds. A quick stroke upwards towards the unprotected groin was a favourite manoeuvre, and a monk on horseback would stand up in his stirrups and whirl the naginata about him.

There is a famous account of naginata fighting by a warrior monk during the first battle of Uji in 1180. The planks of the bridge over the River Uji had been removed as a defence, but the nimble sōhei climbed on to the beams of the bridge, and whirled his naginata like a propeller, deflecting the arrows that were fired at him:

Then Gochin-no-Tajima, throwing away the sheath of his long naginata, strode forth alone on to the bridge, whereupon the Heike straightaway shot at him fast and furious. Tajima, not at all perturbed, ducking to avoid the higher ones and leaping up over those that flew low, cut through those that flew straight with his whirring naginata, so that even the enemy looked on in admiration. Thus it was that he was dubbed 'Tajima the arrow-cutter'.

Later in the same account Tajima is replaced on the bridge by his comrade Jomyō, who illustrates the individual fighting skills of the sōhei in no uncertain fashion:

With his naginata he mows down five of the enemy, but with the sixth the naginata snaps asunder in their midst, and flinging it away he draws his tachi, wielding it in the zig-zag style, the interlacing, cross, reversed dragonfly, waterwheel and eight-sides-at-once styles of sword fighting, thus cutting down eight men; but as he brought down the ninth with an exceedingly mighty blow on the helmet the blade snapped at the hilt and fell with a splash into the water beneath. Then, seizing his tantō, which was the only weapon he had left, he plied it as one in a death fury.

The other weapon the monks carried was the fear of the gods they represented. Every monk carried the Buddhist form of 'rosary beads', and would readily pronounce a curse upon anyone who offended him. The Imperial Court were particularly vulnerable to such treatment, as their lives were conducted according to strict religious and astrological rules, and Mount Hiei was of course their spiritual guardian. Often the monks would reinforce their presence by carrying down into Kyōto the sacred omikoshi. Omikoshi are very elaborate portable shrines, and can be seen today whenever there is a shrine festival in Japan. They are associated with the Shintō religion rather than Buddhism, but in the time of the warrior monks Shintō and Buddhism were closely related, and when the monk Saichō had founded the Mount Hiei temples in 788 he had dedicated them to the Shintō god (or kami) called Sannō, the 'King of the Mountain', who was already worshipped there. Sannō's shrine was the Hiyoshi Shrine at the foot of Mount Hiei, and when the monks headed for the capital they would call in at the Hiyoshi Shrine and collect the omikoshi, into which would be ritually transferred the mitama (spirit) of Sannō. The omikoshi was carried on poles by about twenty monks, exactly as festival shrines are transported nowadays, and any assault on

Right: The traditional costume of the sōhei (monk soldier or warrior monk) is depicted here on a modern print of Benkei, the most famous warrior monk of all. He wears a monk's cowl and black outer robe over a dō-maru armour. He carries a naginata, and wears geta (clogs) on his feet, which would not have been a practical proposition for fighting.

the omikoshi was regarded as an offence to the kami Sannō himself. The Heike Monogatari, the great epic of the twelfth century wars, describes several incidents when the omikoshi of Sannō was taken to Kyōto. One incursion resulted from the murder of a Mount Hiei monk by a courtier. The shrine of the Mountain King was taken down to Kyōto, and the monks chanted the six hundred volumes of the Dai Hannya Kyō (a Buddhist sutra) as a curse. Sometimes the omikoshi would be left in the streets while the monks returned to the mountain. Here it would remain, to the dread of all the citizens, until the monks' desires were satisfied. This subtle form of blackmail was first used in 1082.

Sōhei and Samurai

Townspeople and courtiers, therefore, could be thoroughly intimidated by these monk warriors, but for much of their history their main energies were directed at each other, because it did not take the temples long to realise that their sōhei could also be useful in disputes between various temples and subdivisions of temples. It is important to realise that these squabbles were not religious wars as we know them, but they were just as fierce and ruthless, and the issue was frequently settled by burning down a few of the opposing temple's buildings. Alliances were regularly formed, and as easily broken. In spite of their relationship and proximity, Enryaku-ji and Miidera maintained deep rivalry and jealousy of each other, and were always ready to fight. We hear of them united against the Kōfuku-ji of Nara in 1081, when Kōfuku-ji burned Miidera and carried off much loot, but later in the same year Enryaku-ji burned Miidera over a succession dispute. In 1113 Enryaku-ji burned the Kiyomizudera in Kyōto over a rival appointment of an abbot, and in 1140 attacked Miidera again. However, 'The Mountain' would always rally round if one of its branch temples was attacked by samurai or Nara sōhei, and such an incident in 1117 is described in the Heike Monogatari, which quotes the sad words of the ex-Emperor Go Shirakawa-In:

There are three things which are beyond my control: the rapids on the Kamo river, the dice at gambling, and the monks of the mountain.

On a later occasion the defiant sōhei advanced on the capital carrying the omikoshi of the Mountain King, and 'as they entered Ichijō (a street in Kyōto) from the eastern side, people wondered if the sun and moon had not fallen from heaven'. They marched through the city to the Imperial Palace where they found an armed guard of samurai and foot soldiers barring their way at the northern gate. The samurai were under the command of Minamoto Yorimasa who was later to fight shoulder to shoulder with the warrior monks at the Battle of Uji. He showed great respect to the sacred omikoshi:

Then Yorimasa quickly leapt from his horse, and taking off his helmet and rinsing his mouth with water, made humble obeisance before the sacred emblem, all his three hundred retainers likewise following his example.

The monks hesitated in their attack, noting the presence of the respected (and respectful) Yorimasa, and his comparatively small army, and decided to attack another gate instead. Here no diplomatic general was waiting for them, but a hail of arrows from mounted samurai:

a struggle ensued, for the samurai drew their bows and shot at them so that many arrows struck the sacred omikoshi of Juzenji and some of the priests were killed. Many of their followers were wounded, the noise of the shouts and groaning even ascending to the heights of the Bonten paradise, while Kenro-Chijin, the mighty Earth-deity, was struck with consternation. Then the priestly bands, leaving their omikoshi at the gate, fled back lamenting to their temples.

The incident had shown that the monks could be faced down. It was also an indication that the samurai were by no means as frightened of the monks as were the courtiers. In 1146 a young samurai named Taira Kiyomori had his first dramatic clash with the sōhei. On the day of the Gion Festival in Kyōto one of Kiyomori's attendants quarrelled with a priest from the Gion shrine. Vowing revenge, Kiyomori led an attack on the Gion shrine while their own omikoshi was being paraded. With a haughty samurai disregard for religious scruples, Kiyomori himself deliberately shot an arrow at the omikoshi, which struck the gong on the front, and proclaimed the act of sacrilege far and near. Enraged at this offence to an omikoshi, 7,000 warrior monks from Mount Hiei descended on the capital, baying for Kiyomori's blood. But by now the Imperial Court had become dependent upon samurai armies such as those of Kiyomori's Taira clan for defending them against all incursions, including monastic ones. Kiyomori's continued support was therefore more important than placating the monks, and they exonerated Kiyomori on payment of a nominal fine.

Few incidents illustrate the rise of the samurai as a power in the land better than Kiyomori's personal defiance. With one arrow a samurai leader had burst the bubble of monastic pretensions. Through this act the power of the Taira family grew, and the influence of the monks began to decline, until both were swallowed up in the Gempei War.

Below: Armoured sōhei of the Kōfuku-ji at Nara defend their temple against the Taira army.

Indeed, it may be that but for the war the story of the warrior monks would have been virtually at an end. The samurai clans were willing to face them militarily, and, more importantly, to challenge the religious power they claimed to have, so with the coming of war the opportunity arose to neutralise both sources of monastic influence.

The Sōhei in the Gempei War

From about 1180 onwards the activities of the warrior monks became submerged in the Gempei civil war, in which the defiant Taira Kiyomori was one of the chief protagonists. His rivals, the Minamoto clan, had acquired the services of a pretender to the throne, a certain Prince Mochihito, who raised a rebellion against the Taira in 1180. The reaction was swift, and Prince Mochihito fled to the temple of Miidera and its monk armies, pursued by Taira samurai. Miidera sent out appeals for help to the Enryaku-ji and the temples of Kyōto, but despite his previous insult to the monks in 1146 Kiyomori managed to ensure the Enryaku-ji's neutrality by a handsome bribe. Nor was the Kōfuku-ji of Nara inclined to help its northern rivals, and left Miidera alone to face the Taira army. The monks and the Minamoto samurai retreated across the Uji river, and tore up the planking of the bridge as a defence. This led to the Battle of Uji, and the incident of Tajima the Arrow Cutter described above, but despite the bravery shown by monks fighting across a broken bridge the rebellion failed, and the monks of Miidera were not allowed to forget their unfortunate alliance. Taira Tomomori, one of Kiyomori's sons, led the counter-attack on Miidera.

> At the monastery about a thousand sōhei, arming themselves, made a shield barrier, threw up a barricade of felled trees, and awaited them. At the Hour of the Hare they began to draw their bows, and the battle continued the whole day, until when evening came three hundred of the monks and their men had fallen. Then the fight went on in the darkness, and the Imperial army forced its way into the monastery and set it on fire.

Much worse was in store for the temples of Nara. They may not have actively supported the rebellion, but neither had they opposed it. Kiyomori had sent envoys to negotiate an

THE SECOND BATTLE OF KIZUGAWAGUCHI, 1578

Japanese warships of the Sengoku Period were clumsy and primitive compared to contemporary European vessels. In this picture we see one of Oda Nobunaga's specially commissioned, extra-large ōadake-bune ships, built for him by his admiral Kuki Yoshitaka. It is taking on a standard-sized ōadake-bune of the Mōri navy, which kept open the supply lines for Nobunaga's hated enemies, the Buddhist fanatics of the Ikkō-ikki. The ships resemble two floating yagura, or wooden castles. The whole surface, called the tate ita, was covered with planking 6–10 centimetres thick. Along the four sides loopholes were cut for guns and bows, leaving no dead space that was not covered by defensive fire. As well as the advantage given by their extra size, the Oda ships were also reinforced in some way with iron. It is unlikely that they were covered with iron sheets, which would have made them 'ironclad battleships', though a certain priest saw the ships as they put to sea, and describes these magnificent vessels as 'iron-ships'. A European visitor was very impressed by their firepower. Kuki Yoshitaka had a chance to test them when he encountered a pirate fleet as he rounded the coast of the Kii peninsula. The pirates opened fire, but were soon dispersed. He then sailed the six iron ships into Osaka bay, escorted by smaller vessels.

At this second Battle of Kizugawaguchi the Mōri fleet was outclassed. Nobunaga's battleships took the fight to them, and had the satisfaction of seeing arrows and musket-balls bouncing off their ships. The engagement developed into hand-to-hand fighting as the ships came alongside and boarding-parties fought each other. Several Mōri vessels were burned or sunk, but one of Nobunaga's iron ships was lost when it was boarded and simply capsized, showing one fundamental disadvantage of the style.

alliance with the Taira clan, but the monks most unwisely assaulted the messengers and forcibly shaved their heads, then added insult to injury by making a wooden head which they called the head of Kiyomori, and played football with it in the temple courtyard. Kiyomori still behaved with caution, and sent a force of five hundred men with orders to use no violence unless absolutely necessary. The deputation was attacked by the monks, sixty samurai were killed, and their heads displayed around the pool of Sarusawa opposite the southern gate of the Kōfuku-ji. Furious at the reaction, Kiyomori immediately sent his son Shigehira with orders to subdue the whole city of Nara. When the monks heard of his approach they made ready to defend their temples and the city. Ditches were dug and palisades erected, and from these flimsy barricades they faced the Taira army.

Shigehira's mounted samurai bowmen were held off until dark by the determined monks. There were no niceties of samurai combat, for the monkish rabble were unworthy of a challenge. Yet no cavalry charge could break through, so the fateful order was given to use that most deadly of weapons in the samurai armoury – fire. It is probable that

Shigehira only intended to burn down a few isolated buildings to break the monks' defensive line, as rival temples had done to one another for two centuries, but a particularly strong wind was blowing. Despite the monks' efforts to save it, the Kōfuku-ji temple was reduced to ashes. The flames spread to the great Tōdai-ji, whose Daibutsudan (Great Buddha Hall) housed the enormous statue of Buddha.

In all, 3,500 people died in the burning of Nara, and of the original buildings only the Imperial Repository of the Shōsō-In remains to this day. The heads of 1,000 monks who were killed were displayed in Nara or carried back to Kyōto. The punishment of Nara sent a chill through Mount Hiei, and when in 1183 the Minamoto leader Kiso Yoshinaka entered Enryaku-ji the monks sheltered him for a while, but took no part in his military campaigns. For the rest of the Gempei War the monks remained subdued, and played no further part in the fighting.

The Revival of the Sōhei

It was to be almost two hundred years before monk armies again became a force to be reckoned with in Japanese politics. Nara was

Left: The monks of Nara attempt to extinguish the flames during the attack by the Taira troops.

Right: A sōhei mounted on a horse, and wearing the monk's cowl over his armour.

rebuilt by the victorious Minamoto, but was never again to feel the clash of battle. Indeed the following incident from the Azuma Kagami account of the Shōkyū War of 1221 shows how far the monks of Nara had retreated from the days of sōhei armies. The Nara monks had provided refuge for the rebels, and faced retribution:

Tokifusa and Yasutoki mustered several thousand warriors from the capital and adjacent provinces ... and sent them off towards Nara. News of this caused great consternation among the priests ... 'If warriors enter Nara, the result will be the same as when the Taira burned down the great temples ...' Moved by their frantic pleas, the warriors returned to the capital.

Mount Hiei remained quiet during the Shōkyū War, but during the Nambokuchō Wars of the fourteenth century it provided a refuge for the son of Emperor Go-Daigo. He is known to history as the 'Prince of the Great Pagoda', and the warrior monks were his first allies. Accounts of his operations show monk armies as well-armed and confident as their predecessors, and also as unsuccessful. In the Taiheiki, which deals with the wars of the fourteenth century, there is a vivid account of a single combat between a monk armed with a naginata and a mounted samurai:

> Just then a monk kicked over the shield in front of him and sprang forward, whirling his naginata like a water wheel. It was Kajitsu of Harima. Kaitō received him with his right arm, meaning to cut down into his helmet bowl, but the glancing sword struck down lightly from Kajitsu's shoulder-plate to the cross stitching at the bottom of his armour. Again Kaitō struck forcefully, but his left foot broke through its stirrup, and he was likely to fall from his horse, As he straightened his body, Kajitsu thrust up his naginata, and two or three times drove its point quickly into his helmet. Kaitō fell off his horse, pierced cleanly through the throat. Swiftly Kajitsu put down his foot on Kaitō's armour, seized his side hair, and cut off his head, that he might fix it to his naginata. Rejoicing, he mocked the enemy.

Battles involving warrior monks, however, are few and far between. On the occasion of an incursion to Kyōto by the monks of Mount Hiei, the samurai defenders use their skill as mounted archers to harass the monks, most of whom are on foot. Arrows are fired as horsemen gallop up and retire, until the resolve of the sōhei is worn away:

> The monks went out before the west gate of the temple, a mere thousand men, unsheathing their weapons and battling against the enemy drawing near. But these pulled back their horses and retreated nimbly when the monks attacked, and galloped round to the rear when the monks stood in their places, as it was planned from the beginning. Thus they galloped and harassed them six or seven times, until at length the bodies of the monks grew weary, by reason that they fought on foot and wore heavy armour. Seizing the advantage, the warriors sent forward archers to shoot them mercilessly.

As the samurai close in on them the naginata finally come into their own for a last-ditch struggle:

> So they spoke, whirling their great four shaku-long [1.5m] naginata like water wheels. Again and again they leaped and attacked with flying sparks of fire. Many were the warriors whose horses' legs were cut when they sought to smite these two. Many were those who fell to the ground and perished with smashed helmets!

Yet all these heroics were to no avail, and the sōhei were crushed as effectively as their predecessors had been.

In conclusion, therefore, it can be seen that the warrior monks were at their most influential when dealing with superstitious courtiers or ignorant townsfolk. In disputes between temples their fighting skills came into their own, but were to prove no match for the samurai. Perhaps the greatest compliment the Taira were to give them was to recognise their potential for military rivalry, but then to destroy them so utterly that it was to take two centuries for them to recover, only to fail again in the harsh world of samurai warfare.

Below: Akamatsu Enshin (1277–1371), a samurai and fervent member of the Zen sect (he is wearing a monk's cowl), who fought for Emperor Go-Daigo, but later supported the Ashikaga Shōgun.

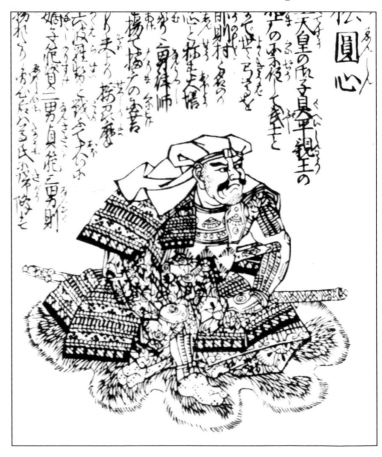

Chapter 4

SAMURAI WARFARE IN TRANSITION

Below: This exquisite ivory carving shows two samurai dressed in simple dō-maru engaging in a one-to-one grappling fight. One has a tantō (dagger) tied securely at his belt, and he carries his sword in his left hand.

With the ending of the Gempei War Japan entered a time of comparative peace, broken sporadically by fierce wars, until the whole country was engulfed in the Sengoku-jidai (The Age of the Country at War). Military advances progressed in leaps and bounds during the times of hostilities, enabling samurai warfare to reach its peak in the Sengoku times. So much development took place during that final century of conflict that all subsequent chapters will be devoted entirely to it. This chapter will present a historical overview of the intervening four centuries, highlighting important developments in warfare as and when they occur.

The Kamakura Period and the Mongol Invasions

The style of samurai warfare discussed in the previous chapters enabled the samurai, as the military class, to come to power in Japan when Minamoto Yoritomo, the victor of the Gempei War, became the first permanent Shōgun, as military dictator. The status and power was not to be confined within the same lineage, however. Yoritomo did not live long to enjoy his triumph, but was killed in 1192 following a riding accident. His death was a great shock to the Minamoto, and effectively their end as a ruling house, for they managed to provide only two more Shōguns, both of whom were firmly under the control of Yoritomo's widow's family, the Hōjō. Yet so firmly entrenched was the new notion of the hereditary Shogūnate (the bakufu) that the Hōjō accepted that they could not become Shōgun, because they were not descended from the Minamoto, and instead supplied ten Regents between 1199 and 1333. The capital of the Hōjō was Kamakura, so Kyōto was relegated to the status of the Emperor's home. All the important decisions were made in Kamakura, set in the heartlands of the fierce Eastern Warriors. The century and a half between 1192 and 1333 is known as the 'Kamakura Period'.

It began with a time of comparative peace. There was an attempt to restore the Emperor's power, but the revolt was crushed by the Hōjō samurai, and little disturbed Japan until 1274 when the calm was shattered by the first of two attempts by the Mongol Emperor of China, Kublai Khan, grandson of Genghis Khan, to invade Japan. It is much to the credit of the samurai that both landings, the second taking place in 1281, were repulsed so totally. The circumstances surrounding both wars against the Mongol invaders have been obscured by the coup de grâce delivered on both occasions by the weather, the latter storm being so sudden and so fierce that it was immediately dubbed the kami-kaze or 'Divine Tempest', sent by the Sun-Goddess to aid her people. Decisive though the typhoon was, it would have been minimal in its effectiveness if the determination and fighting qualities of the samurai had not forced the entire fleet to lie at anchor with all their armies on board, cooped up by the ferocity of Japanese raids in little ships, and unable to establish a beachhead because of the tenacity with which the land was defended. The samurai, although outnumbered, not only held their ground but took the battle to the Mongol ships.

The Mongol invasion force consisted of Mongol troops, and thousands of impressed Koreans and Chinese, whose ships were used to transport the armada to Japan. Their initial assault caused great alarm because the Mongols' manner of fighting was so different from that of the Japanese. Instead of valuing individual combat, they fired huge salvoes of arrows and attacked in phalanxes of spearmen. They also launched exploding firebombs by catapult.

A further shock produced by the Mongols was that their ways conflicted with the tradition in which the young samurai warriors were steeped, which was one of individual honour and prowess, supported by precedent and myth going back two centuries. The notion of individual combat, of the giving and receiving of challenges, were all in their stock-in-trade, and suddenly they were faced with this alien enemy, with no common language in which challenges could be delivered, and a foreign tradition of non-élite archers who shot arrows by the hundred in massed volleys. The earlier chapter which dealt with the reality of warfare during the Heian Period, however, makes it most unlikely that a situation ever occurred where samurai warriors stood in dumbfounded silence, unable to fight the enemy because language difficulties prevented them from issuing challenges. The hail of arrows must have surprised them, but what stood the samurai in good stead was the now well-developed tradition of fighting in mutually supportive small units. After the shock of the first encounter on the beaches of Kyushu, the samurai rallied, dismounting from their horses when necessary and engaging the swarms of Mongol warriors in hand-to-hand combat, where their sharp swords dug into the foreigners' armoured coats.

When the Mongols returned in 1281 the Japanese were better prepared. Defensive walls had been erected, and daring bands of samurai took the fight to the Mongol ships in hit-and-run raids. But this second invasion was being conducted by an army many times larger than the Japanese defence force, and all looked hopeless until the kami-kaze blew up and smashed the Mongol fleet as it lay at anchor. During the Second World War the suicide pilots who tried to hold back the American invasion identified themselves with the wind that destroyed the Mongols, and called themselves kami-kaze.

Samurai as Guerrilla

A century later the ruling Emperor Go-Daigo tried to restore the old Imperial power. The current Regent was Hōjō Takatoki (1303–33) who took over the shikken at the age of eight, but grew up to be of poor intelligence and weak morals. It was no doubt Takatoki's reputation that encouraged Go-Daigo to try his hand, and Go-Daigo's raising of the flag of revolt against their decadent Regency found many takers. To be seen to have helped a grateful Emperor against an unpopular Regency would be a likely source of reward and privilege.

In samurai tradition the greatest principle of all was loyalty to one's master, and one samurai who supported Go-Daigo when the revolt began, and continued to be loyal even when things were going against the Emperor's cause, was Kusunoki Masashige. Masashige held out against bakufu troops from a succession of mountain fortresses, and kept up his resistance in spite of Go-Daigo's being captured by the bakufu and a rival Emperor being enthroned in his stead. This happened in 1332. Go-Daigo was exiled to the island of Oki, and the Kemmu Restoration, as his action was called, looked as though it were over.

All would indeed have been lost had not Kusunoki Masashige continued his resistance in the form of a guerrilla campaign among the mountains of Yoshino. In 1333 three armies left Kamakura to destroy his latest hideouts, and defeated Kusunoki's comrade-in-arms Prince Morinaga, Go-Daigo's son. But Kusunoki Masashige withdrew to another fortress called Chihaya, deep in the mountains and forests of Kawachi province and much stronger than Akasaka. Chihaya held out against every attempt to take it, in a classic siege that is a notable event in samu-

Right: The statue of Kusunoki Masashige outside the Imperial Palace in Tokyo.

rai history. The continued resistance at Chihaya inspired Go-Daigo to return from exile and try again.

Another samurai leader, Nitta Yoshisada, then took up arms for the Emperor, and led an army against Kamakura. He attacked the city through the passes in the hills that surround it, but no impression was made on the defence until Yoshisada was able to launch a surprise attack round the cape of Inamuragasaki. Legend credits this success to divine intervention. He is supposed to have thrown his sword into the sea as an offering to the Sun-Goddess, at which the waters parted before his army. The Emperor's army flooded into Kamakura, and fierce fighting took place in the streets. Eventually the last of the Hōjō shikken retired to a temple on the outskirts of Kamakura called the Tōshō-ji, an ironic name as it means 'the temple of victory in the East'. In a cave behind the Tōshō-ji they committed suicide.

Many of their supporters were less fortunate. We noted in a previous chapter that samurai were always supported by scores of common foot soldiers. Following the fall of Kamakura the bodies of these men were buried in grave pits in the Zaimokusa district of Kamakura, where the fiercest fighting had taken place. These grave pits have recently been excavated, and the study of the remains by archaeologists confirms the cutting power of the Japanese sword and the lack of head protection worn by common soldiers. There are skulls that have been pierced by the points of swords, others that have been cut by the edge of the blade, an eloquent testimony to the now legendary weapon of the samurai.

The fall of Kamakura confirmed Go-Daigo as Emperor, but his reign was to be brief. The idea of a Shōgun, a military dictator from the samurai class, was a very appealing one for samurai warlords, and one of Go-Daigo's supporters was descended from the Minamoto, the only family that could supply a Shōgun. This man, Ashikaga Takauji, seized power, and became the first Ashikaga Shōgun, ruling under a rival Emperor whom he appointed. The Nambokuchō Wars, the 'War Between the Courts', continued for the next fifty years, with Go-Daigo and his successors 'ruling' from the above-mentioned mountains of Yoshino. Here the Kusunoki family continued to serve Go-Daigo loyally. Their greatest member, Kusunoki Masashige, was killed in 1336 at the Battle of Minatogawa, a pitched battle rather than the type of siege at which he excelled. Even though he knew his cause was hopeless, Kusunoki Masashige went proudly to his death in service of the Emperor. Before he left for Minatogawa, Kusunoki Masashige bade farewell to his young son Masatsura, and asked him to continue the struggle in the name of the Emperor. This Masatsura did valiantly from the hills of Yoshino, until he was forced to leave the security the mountains provided to repel a challenge from the Ashikaga army. Before leaving, he and his men paid homage at the tomb of Emperor Go-Daigo, who had died in exile, then Masatsura wrote a farewell poem on the temple door with an arrowhead. He was killed in the fight that followed, the Battle of Shijo-Nawate in 1348.

Development in Arms and Armour

During this period armour changed only in detail from the styles of the Gempei War, and

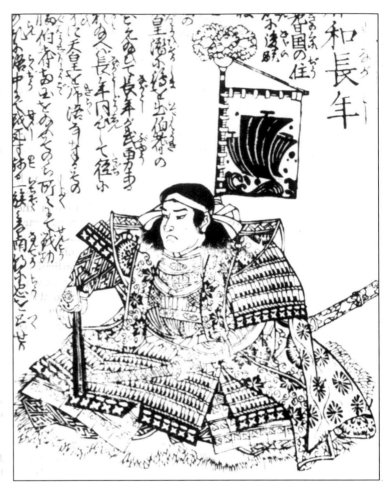

Above: Nawa Nagatoshi, a supporter of Emperor Go-Daigo. The inclusion of a sashimono banner is incorrect for the period.

the ōyoroi armour attained its final decorative form. Many of the suits of armour that have survived to this day were made during the Kamakura Period. They are often of superlative construction, with many decorative features such as kuwagata, the 'antlers' at the front of the helmet. It is also during the Kamakura Period that we meet one of the most famous of all swordsmiths, Masamune, whose work became legendary. It is from the efforts of such craftsmen as Masamune that the art of making the Japanese sword acquired the mystique it retains to this day.

During this period there is a noticeable decline in the use of the bow by samurai, yet there is no clear relationship between the abandonment of the bow and the adoption of the sword. Both required the same dedication, training and capital expense that only samurai could afford. But during this period the samurai as a mounted archer gradually fades from view. To some extent this trend was forced by the Nambokuchō Wars which

Below: Kusunoki Masashige bids farewell to his son Masatsura before going off to the Battle at Minatogawa in 1336. Masatsura swore to uphold the cause of the Emperor Go-Daigo, and met his death at the Battle of Shijō-Nawate in 1348. Masashige is in 'undress' armour, with a yoroi-hitatare (armour robe), and the left kote (sleeve) only, shown tied under his armpit. His other arm would be left free for drawing the bow. The rest of Masashige's armour is in the chest behind him. (Reproduced by courtesy of the Nanpian Kannon-ji, Kawachi-Nagano)

were fought over wooded and hilly terrain. Much more fighting had to be done on foot, the long wars in the mountains making horses useful only for transporting a warrior to the battlefield. The limitations of the box-like yoroi for activities other than archery became more acute, and the yoroi style of armour was gradually phased out in favour of the foot soldiers' dō-maru. One small detail of samurai costume shows how bows were becoming less important, because the samurai began to wear armour on both sleeves, and developed much better protection for the thighs (the haidate) and the calves (the suneate). The helmet's neck guard (the shikoro) was now made much flatter, enabling the wearer to swing his sword around more easily. This was particularly necessary in the case of the extra-long sword called the nodachi, which was popular at this time. It was held by two hands and swung in wide circles. A nodachi is being described in the following section from the Taiheiki:

...an enemy warrior called Saji Magorō, a resident of the province of Tamba, brought his horse up sideways in front of the west gate and easily slashed the bellies of three enemies with his five-shaku [1.7m] sword, such a long sword as has never been seen before. Then this warrior struck his sword against the

door of the gate, straightening it where it had bent a little, and turned his horse's head to face the enemy.

As for other weapons, we read of many samurai using the monk's naginata, and as the fifteenth century begins there is a gradual change towards the straight spear. An early written account confirming its use appears in the Onin no ki (the Chronicle of Onin):

Ichijō Masafusa, grandson of the retired Regent, was sojourning in Hyōgo, where he had his estates ... Any crude barbarian should have recognised him as an exalted personage. Yet on the seventh day of the tenth month of 1469 some warrior, without pausing to think, assumed that Masafusa was an enemy and ran a long spear through his breast.

The development of spears will be considered in more detail in the chapter which follows.

The Taiheiki accounts often reflect the changing nature of samurai warfare. There are long descriptions of sieges, which will be discussed later, a topic almost entirely missing from the Heike Monogatari, and in contrast to its paeans for noble warriors such as Kusunoki Masashige, the Taiheiki recognises the existence of akutō (evil) bands of lawless

Left: The defence of Chihaya castle by the samurai of Kusunoki Mas-ashige. Note the use of dummy troops to draw the attackers' fire.

guerrilla bandits. They are able to withstand sieges, and obey no rules in warfare.

Following the Wars Between the Courts there were several small scale rebellions against the Ashikaga Shōguns, until a bitter dispute between two rival clans burst into a civil war that was to have disastrous consequences. The Onin War, which began in the First Year of Onin, 1467 according to the Japanese calendar, has a unique place in samurai history, as the capital itself was the battleground. The clans fought it out with bow, sword, spear and naginata in the streets of Kyōto, which were soon reduced to blackened wastes. Apart from the deployment of straight spears, the fighting was little different from that of earlier times:

> ... they let loose volley after volley of arrows and cut the attackers down. All of the leading troops fell ... Neither shield nor armour could withstand the merciless barrage of arrows poured forth from the approach to the thicket.

As the war spread to the provinces other families realised that the Shōgun no longer possessed any power, and Japan split into a country of competing warlords. One development was the enormous increase in the numbers of men who were likely to be drawn into conflict. As well as the irregular bands noted above, there was an important development in the use of foot soldiers. Men were recruited casually, and referred to as

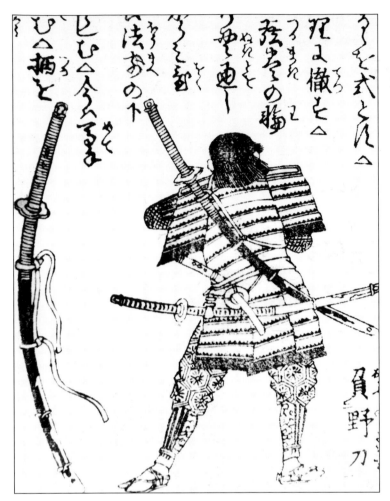

Above: A nodachi (long sword) slung on a samurai's back.

Left: A samurai demonstrates fine swordplay as his opponents try to dislodge him from a statue.

(which now included disciplined foot soldiers), the introduction of firearms and the development of castles.

The erroneous impression is frequently given that following the Onin War Japan sunk into chaos. There may always have been wars going on during this time, but it was not a state of total war. The overall feature of the Sengoku Period was the absence of any firm central control. The Ashikaga Shōgun had little power, yet enough remained with the institution to make the competing warlords desirous of obtaining the position for their own families, if their lineage allowed it. Alternatively, should their lineage rule out the first place, to rule through a nominal Shōgun was the height of personal ambition. Thus Toyotomi Hideyoshi, the son of a woodcutter from what is now Nagoya, became the first man unquestionably to rule the whole of Japan in centuries. While he lived his power was unchallenged, and even though there had not been a Shōgun for nearly thirty years Hideyoshi had sufficient political acumen to realise that to take the title for himself would lose him more support than it would gain. So he followed the example of the Hōjō family and became Regent. By contrast, the Tokugawa, who followed him, had an impeccable lineage back to the Minamoto, so through Tokugawa Ieyasu the Shōgunate was revived and lasted 250 years.

The other myth concerning the Sengoku Period concerns the activities of the Sengoku Daimyō themselves. The word Daimyō means 'great name'. 'Warlords' is a convenient English expression which conveys something of their role, but they were not bandit leaders. Once power had been achieved it was consolidated through economic means as much as through fighting. Good government, and a fair treatment of the peasantry, who could easily abscond to till the fields of a rival, was as much the hallmark of the successful Daimyō as military skill. War was certainly one of the major means by which they achieved their own local power, but being born to the correct set of parents was another way to prominence, because many of the Sengoku Daimyō were no more than the legitimate heirs of ancient families. The Shimazu of Satsuma, the Matsuura of Hirado, and the Mōri of the Inland Sea are all examples of continuity of power within a family in the grand samurai tradition. The difference which the Sengoku

ashigaru ('light feet'). Their widespread and sometimes uncontrolled use contradicted much of the samurai ideal of élite combat, but large numbers had to be used by any successful samurai leader. The ashigaru took full use of the opportunity provided by casual recruitment in a situation of chaos, and looted and burned indiscriminately, adding considerably to the misery of the Onin War.

The Rise of the Sengoku Daimyō

The Onin War ushered in a century and a half during which hardly a year passed without a battle or campaign being fought somewhere in Japan. The term the Sengoku Jidai, or 'The Age of the Country at War', is commonly used as an epithet for this violent age. For the first fifty years following the Onin War techniques of samurai warfare hardly developed, but just before the middle of the sixteenth century it entered a rapid period of change, spurred on by the use of large armies

今上 衣スク甲丁言

Left: It was during the Kamakura Period that the samurai sword reached its peak of technological perfection. Here it is wielded in typical two-handed style by one of the 'Forty-Seven Loyal Retainers' in a print by Kuniyoshi.

Right: Gamō Katahide (1534–84), keeper of Hino castle for the Sasaki, who later served Oda Nobunaga.

Right: The celebrated single combat fought between Uesugi Kenshin and Takeda Shingen at the fourth Battle of Kawanakajima in 1561. (Courtesy of Christie's)

Period gave to this particular generation of a noble line was the freedom to exercise that power by defending against enemies, and acquiring more territory. There was simply no one around to tell them to stop, apart from other daimyō who may have had similar ambitions.

For much of the Sengoku Period the provinces controlled by the Sengoku Daimyō were quite well defined and ruled as a stable economic unit. There is little evidence of civil war within these territories except where the Ikkō-ikki sectarians were involved. Warfare tended to be confined to clashes between daimyō, particularly at sensitive areas where two territories met. Thus the border between the Takeda, Uesugi and Hōjō lands was frequently contested. Kawanakajima, an area of flatland which was effectively a no man's land for the Takeda and Uesugi, saw no fewer than five battles across its fields. It was such conflicts, coupled with their geographical remoteness from the capital, that acted as a counterweight to whatever pretensions these daimyō might have had to becoming Shōgun. Many possessed the necessary military power, but few were fated to exercise it in this direction.

The exceptions included the three great unifiers of Japan. The first to take the country down this road was Oda Nobunaga (1534–82), a daimyō from Owari province. Nobunaga was a military genius who had that most precious of qualities – the ability to benefit from his own mistakes. Having learned hard lessons at the hands of the Ikkō-ikki sectarians, Nobunaga applied some military techniques acquired from them, and added others gleaned from European traders. His career was at the peak of its success when he was murdered by one of his own generals. Within thirteen days Nobunaga was avenged by another of his generals, Toyotomi Hideyoshi (1539–98), who crushed the traitor in the battle of Yamazaki, and inherited Nobunaga's gains. Hideyoshi completed the subjugation of rivals with campaigns against Shikoku island and the invasion of the southern island of Kyushu, then sent a Japanese army to invade Korea in 1592. But Toyotomi Hideyoshi died in the manner all dictators dread, leaving an infant son to inherit. Civil war again broke out, resulting in a complete victory for Tokugawa Ieyasu (1542–1616) at the battle of Sekigahara in 1600.

When Tokugawa Ieyasu became Shōgun in 1603 young Toyotomi Hideyori was brushed aside, but by 1614 two things had changed. Hideyori had grown to manhood, and Ieyasu's victory at Sekigahara had left a vast pool of unemployed rōnin, a word that means literally 'men of the waves' – unemployed samurai thrown on to the military scrapheap. Toyotomi Hideyori also still possessed the family seat of Osaka castle, which had the potential to become an alternative power base to that of the new Shōgun, whose headquarters were located in Edo, the little fishing village which is now the city of Tokyo. The siege of Osaka castle, described later as a case study, brought the Sengoku Period to an end. The following sections describe techniques of samurai warfare during these turbulent times.

Above: Toyotomi Hideyoshi, the unifier of Japan, as seen in this effigy of him at Nikkō, where he appears as an archer of the Nara Period.

Left: Details of the stones in a castle wall are clearly seen in this picture of two ninja climbing Iga-Ueno castle, at the city's annual 'Ninja Festival'!

Part Two

THE TECHNIQUES OF SAMURAI WARFARE

Chapter 5

SAMURAI WARFARE IN THE SENGOKU PERIOD

The military power exercised by the Sengoku daimyō from about 1530 onwards brought samurai warfare to the peak of its perfection. This chapter will examine the structure of the Sengoku army, where the most visible change was apparent in the use of firearms, and the weaponry of the mounted samurai.

From Mounted Archer to Mounted Spearman

In the Sengoku Period the possession of a horse still tended to indicate a samurai's élite nature, although financial circumstances obliged some to fight on foot, but there was also a major change in his choice of weaponry. Reference was made in the previous chapter to the use of straight spears from about 1450 onwards. Many were employed by ashigaru, but the most important development concerns their adoption by samurai

in preference to bows. An examination of scroll paintings and screens from the fourteenth to sixteenth centuries shows this evolution taking place. The mounted archer, once the definitive samurai warrior, was no more. In his place rode the mounted spearman. The 'Way of Horse and Bow' had somehow become the 'Way of Horse and Spear'.

The samurai of the period from the eleventh century to about the end of the fourteenth had been essentially élite missile troops. We noted earlier the limitations associated with mounted archery, how the angle of fire was restricted, how only a limited number of arrows could be loosed at the opponent, and how the combination of moving target and moving archer made mortal wounds difficult to achieve. These restrictions could be set aside as long as warfare was seen as something carried out between

Below: The young Maeda Toshiie demonstrates his prowess with the long spear from the saddle of a horse. From the Ehon Taikō-ki.

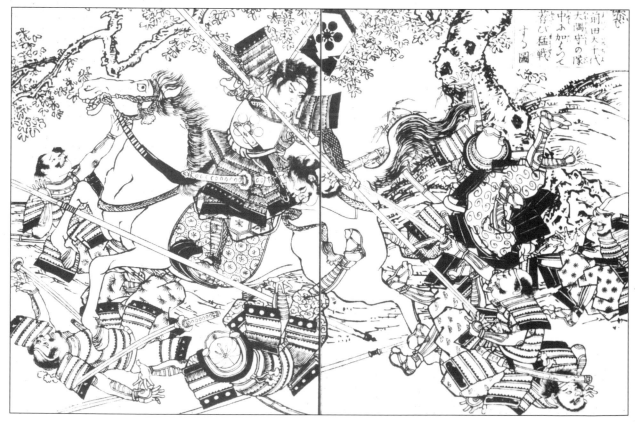

one samurai and another. The role allotted to the genin (warriors' attendants) was one of support, while the samurai, theoretically, did all the fighting. Heads removed through the assistance of a genin would be credited to his master. Such arrangements, accepted by all parties, allowed the niceties of combat to flourish alongside the bitter business of surprise attacks and arson. Even in the most confused epics of the gunkimono there is the overall impression that warfare is really a private matter between two consenting aristocrats.

It was the changes in warfare brought about by the experience of the Mongol invasions and the Nambokuchō Wars that broadened the base of samurai warfare. It became recognised that if the object of the exercise was to bring down a mounted samurai archer then the most efficient way of doing this was not to use another mounted archer, but to set against him half a dozen foot soldiers armed with naginata, kumade (rakes),

or even bows. How, then, was the samurai to defend himself? His arrows would be at their least effective in such a situation, and his sword would have a very limited reach when dealing with foot soldiers, particularly if they were to lure him into the cover of trees and undergrowth, a form of terrain that characterised much of the fighting during the Nambokuchō Wars. The obvious answer was to provide the samurai with a polearm. The naginata, with its curved blade and short handle, was designed for slashing and so was not very practical when wielded from the saddle. The obvious weapon was the straight spear. With a minimum length of about 3 metres, it could be used as a lance or as a slashing weapon as occasion demanded. As a result, by the sixteenth century, illustrations of mounted samurai depict almost exclusively the use of yari (spears) from horseback. There is the occasional naginata, and a few nodachi (extra long swords), a classic example of the latter being the devastation wrought at the Battle of Anegawa in 1570 by the giant Makara Jūrōzaemon, who lopped off limbs and heads as he swung the monstrous weapon from his saddle.

The one option that proved totally impracticable was for the samurai to carry both a bow and a spear. As the following section will demonstrate, samurai still had attendants to serve them, and one would be designated to carry the lord's bow, while another would have the job of carrying the lord's spear. But when the samurai went into battle the spear was his preferred option on nearly all occasions. Samurai carrying bows are hardly ever illustrated or mentioned in chronicles, and the fact that Shimazu Toyohisa carried one with him at the Battle of Sekigahara in 1600 was considered sufficiently unusual for the chronicler to take particular note of it.

Most illustrations show mounted samurai spearmen wearing the more rounded dōmaru armour instead of a yoroi, to which the addition of a solid breastplate was practically the only major change in design during the whole of the Sengoku Period. The warrior now resembled a European knight in all but the addition of the sashimono, an identifying device, frequently a flag, worn on the back of the samurai's armour. The type of spear he carried was called a te-yari (hand spear) or mochi-yari (held spear). The shaft lengths varied between 2 and 2½ ken (between 3.2

Below: Hōjō Sōun (1432–1519) disembarks during one of his early campaigns. He is wearing the monk's cowl. His samurai unload chests and equipment from the boats. From the Hōjō Godaiki.

and 4 metres). Blade lengths varied enormously between about 10 centimetres and 1.5 metres. A fine, if much damaged, specimen of a mochi-yari is preserved in the Sainen-ji, a Jōdo temple in Tokyo. The spear was presented to Hattori Hanzō (1541–96) by Tokugawa Ieyasu, and was then donated to the temple as a votive offering. Hanzō, as well as being one of Ieyasu's most trusted generals, is associated with the ninja of Iga province. The weapon suffered damage during the firebombing of Tokyo in 1945, losing 30 centimetres from its blade, and 150 centimetres from its shaft. Having examined the spear, I have been able to calculate its original dimensions, which are of a shaft length of 3.1 metres, on which was mounted a straight blade that was 5 centimetres wide and 127 centimetres long. The total length of the weapon was therefore 4.38 metres, of which the blade made up just over a quarter. The weight of the remaining parts is 7.5 kilograms, indicating that the original weight was about 12 kilograms.

The size and weight of the Hanzō spear probably indicates an upper limit to the size of a long-bladed spear that could be wielded from a saddle. Longer shafted spears probably had shorter blades, and several specimens exist which have been fitted with cross blades, an example being Katō Kiyomasa's spear preserved in the Hommyō-ji in Kumamoto. Two and a half ken (4m) shafts would have been difficult to use other than as lances or on foot. From the time of Nagashino (1575), when the Takeda cavalry were slaughtered by the Oda matchlockmen, we see an increased reliance on foot fighting by samurai. In the final Battle of Tennōji at the siege of Osaka in 1615, the Tokugawa commanders ordered their samurai to leave their horses at the rear and to go in on foot with spears.

The yari thus gave its bearer the advantage of being a weapon as useful on foot as on horseback. The range of options for samurai were thereby extended from their being élite missile troops to a role of considerable versatility. Spear techniques were developed to enable the samurai to use this weapon in any situation: from horseback, in a charge on foot, or defending castle walls. The yari, therefore, permitted the samurai to defend himself, and take the fight to his enemies, in a way that the exclusive use of a bow had never allowed. The role of the foot soldier as

warrior's assistant continued. The attendant could hand the samurai either bow, spear or even gun when required, while other ashigaru fulfilled the samurai's previous function of missile troops, as we shall see later.

In the painted screen in Hikone castle depicting the Ii family in action at the siege of Osaka castle in 1615, there are several revealing vignettes of a supportive role not unlike the Gempei War. Samurai of the Ii family are charging into the ranks of Kimura Shigenari's army. All have yari except for one character who is running along with a bow. In two separate incidents an Ii samurai is already engaged in hand-to-hand combat with one of the Kimura samurai, and in both cases the servant, who is less elaborately armoured, stands right behind him, and performs the useful function of withdrawing from its socket his master's sashimono, which in this case is a large red flag bearing the samurai's name. The attendant then holds it while the samurai fights. This would

Below: A samurai of the Hōjō, with a very long sword at his belt, fixes his comrade's sashimono flag into the holder on the back of his armour. From the Hōjō Godaiki.

Right: A group of ashigaru, the backbone of samurai armies, showing their simple armour and typical lamp-shade jingasa helmets. From the Ehon Taikō-ki (detail).

have the advantage of allowing the samurai a greater freedom of movement, and would proclaim to the battlefield that a noble struggle was ensuing at that particular location.

The Role and Status of the Ashigaru

The attendants on the Hikone screen are among the members of the Ii army who held the rank of ashigaru, and as the Sengoku Period progressed the ashigaru's role was to become increasingly recognised and increasingly vital. Over the period of a century from the Onin War the ashigaru evolved from a casually recruited, untrained peasant warrior to a soldier with a firm toehold within the samurai hierarchy. At this time, too, there were possibilities of promotion through merit. Toyotomi Hideyoshi started his military career as an ashigaru, and rose within the ranks in a dramatic way that he was later to render almost impossible for others to follow.

The ashigaru therefore became the 'other ranks' of the samurai class, which is how they were to be defined following the establishment of the Tokugawa Shōgunate, when

Left: This small section from a painted screen in Hikone Castle Museum shows the samurai of Ii Naotaka charging against the troops of Kimura Shigenari during the Battle of Wakae, one of the preliminary actions to the Battle of Tennōji in 1615, with which the siege of Osaka castle ended. The Ii soldiers all wear their characteristic red-lacquered armour. The samurai wield long spears, and charge along with their sashimono flags flapping on their backs. Each flag bears the samurai's name.

Right: An okegawa-dō armour, with a solid breastplate. (Courtesy of Christie's)

a firm distinction was drawn between samurai and farmer, and the ashigaru were placed officially within the samurai class. The most striking evidence of their integration is shown on the Ii screen, where we see the daimyō Ii Naotaka's insistence on dressing all his army, including the ashigaru, in red-lacquered armour, yet even this apparent uniformity conceals a certain amount of rank distinction. Close examination reveals that the ashigaru armour is not of the quality worn by the higher ranks of samurai. It was frequently a simple okegawa-dō, consisting of a breastplate and backplate, with kusazuri (tassets) suspended from it. The comman-

der's personal mon (badge) would often be lacquered on to the front. Armoured sleeves might be included, but the ashigaru was unlikely to sport the haidate (thigh guards) or suneate (shin guards) of his betters. The greatest difference in appearance and protection came with the headgear. In place of the samurai's kabuto (helmet) and face mask, the ashigaru wore a simple iron jingasa (war hat), which was usually shaped like a lampshade, and had a cloth neck guard hanging from the rear.

The most profound difference between ashigaru and the higher ranks of samurai was, however, more subtle, and based on

social class, because the samurai possessed surnames, while the ashigaru did not. This curious piece of class distinction is illustrated by the very detailed muster records kept within the Hōjō clan. In 1571 they included a certain Okamoto Hachirōzaemon Masahide, who belonged to the Hōjō daimyō's personal bodyguard (the go-umawari-shū) based at Odawara castle. Okamoto was required to supply a certain number of men to his lord from within his own personal resources, the number of troops being proportional to his income. The record includes the names of the participants. Leading the band is Okamoto himself, plus horse. He is attended by four unmounted samurai, all of whom have surnames and full armour, plus six ashigaru spearmen, two ashigaru flag-bearers, and two others, who would be armoured attendants. In each case the ashigaru's names are recorded simply as 'Genjūrō', 'Shirōzaemon', etc. Prior to about 1615, when such social mobility was still possible, a surname was a most precious acquisition, announcing to the world that you had entered the samurai class. Quite often a former ashigaru would choose as his surname a combination of characters from the name of someone he admired. Toyotomi Hideyoshi is a case in point, choosing an earlier surname of Hashiba from the first character of Shibata Katsuie's name.

The Composition of Samurai Armies

The role of the ashigaru who comprised the specialist weapon units will be discussed in detail in the following chapter. Apart from these men, many ashigaru continued the earlier tradition of the role of warrior's attendant. The two armoured attendants of Okamoto Masahide would no doubt render him a similar personal service to that of the Ii ashigaru on the Osaka screen, and, together with the flag-bearers, indicate that one third of Okamoto's personal fighting strength was given over to what were primarily non-combatant roles, carried out through supporting the samurai in battle, and only fighting themselves when there was an absolute need.

A more detailed study of the make-up of a full Sengoku army confirms this is as the norm, and reveals that such a supportive function of lower-ranking troops, far from having diminished compared to the Gempei War, had in fact increased. To illustrate this we may consider the troops fielded by

Kimata Tosa-no-kami Morikatsu, who commanded the vanguard of the Ii army in about the year 1600. As will be discussed in more detail later, the armies fielded at battles such as Sekigahara consisted of alliances between various clan armies, united by ties of family, vassalage, or remorseless self-interest. The Ii army were fudai (hereditary vassals) of the Tokugawa, and their army traditionally occupied the vanguard of the overall Tokugawa force. The Kimata army therefore held the most glorious place on the samurai bat-

Left: A suit of armour of dō-maru style laced in kebiki-odoshi (close spaced lacing). (Courtesy of Christie's)

tlefield, and one historian has compared the Kimata contingent to the actual tip of a spear blade.

On the authority of the Ii family records, the vanguard commanded by Kimata Morikatsu consisted of 800 men, of whom 90 were Kimata's hatamoto (literally 'under the standard'), his personal bodyguard. These were men whom he furnished from his own income, in the same manner as the more modest figures quoted above for Okamoto. A further breakdown of these 90 shows a considerable supportive function, within a hierarchy which is itself mutually supportive.

The personal service of Kimata Morikatsu, plus:

The Commander's retinue

The lord's personal samurai (kinjū)	4
The lord's personal ashigaru (tomo)	4
Bearer of the lord's cross-bladed spear	1
Bearer of the lord's personal nobori (banner)	1
Groom	1
Sub-total	12

Mounted samurai 3

plus 7 attendants to each, namely:

Samurai	4
Equipment bearers (ashigaru)	2
Groom	1
Sub-total	24

Foot samurai	8
Standard-bearer and attendant	2

Specialised ashigaru

Arquebus	3
Archers	2
Spearmen	4

Servants and general bearers

Lantern-carriers, 4 chests	4
Maku (field curtain) and standards in one large chest	2
Kitchen utensils, 2 chests	2
General porters, 2 packs	2
Food-bearers, 2 packs	2
Packhorse leader	1
Fodder-bearers, 3 packs	3
Grooms with spare horses	2
Gunpowder chest	1
Cloaks, etc., for rainy conditions, 2 large chests	4
The kinjū's armour, 2 large chests	4
The tomo's armour, 1 large chest	2
Another large armour chest	2
The lord's armour, 1 chest	1
Footwear-bearer, 1 chest	1
Arquebuses and tools (bullet moulds, etc.), 1 large chest	2
Bullets, powder, arrows, 1 large chest	2
Sub-total	37

Total 90

Large chests were slung from a pole and carried by two men each, while a 'pack' was of bamboo and straw. All the soldiers would wear the traditional Ii red armour. The Kimata contingent's standard was a large three-dimensional device of cock's feathers. The mounted samurai were important men in their own right, and would have had their names on their sashimono, as would the kinjū in Kimata's personal guard.

Two other men would be attached to the Kimata hatamoto. They are mounted and wear large horō (stiffened cloaks), which distinguish them as tsukai (effectively aides-de-camp) of Ii Naomasa, whose vital functions of communication between Kimata and the rest of the Ii army will be described later. Being mobile, they have no attendants.

By the standards of the Gempei War, therefore, disregarding the specialised weapon troops, the entire body of 90 would appear to contain only four fighting men: the mounted samurai! This was clearly not the case, because the samurai rank no longer depends on the actual use of a horse in battle, and there were ranks within the ashigaru, some having a primary fighting role, tapering down to the unarmoured packhorse drivers, who would only be required to fight in an emergency. Nevertheless, there is still a surprisingly large percentage of the unit whose role is predominately non-combative. The number of baggage-carriers, most of whom have a wakizashi (short sword) as a sidearm, and most of whom are armoured, is 37, which is 41 per cent of the total. In other words, for every primary fighting man (mounted samurai, foot samurai and ashigaru), there is one non-combatant in a supportive role.

Turning to the complete vanguard of 800, of which Kimata's own hatamoto are but one part, our source reveals that of the 800, only 285 are primary combat troops, either mounted or foot, bringing the overall percentage down to 36, which is a surprisingly low figure. In Chapter 1 it was noted that sources for the Heian Period suggest one or more attendants to every mounted samurai. On the evidence of the Okamoto and Kimata records, therefore, the proportion would appear not to have changed greatly. The major difference, of course, is the increased complexity of role and hierarchy within these supportive ranks below the samurai. The shift from samurai as archers to spearmen, the reliance on ashigaru as missile troops, and the longer duration of campaigns, requiring more supplies, are all factors in this development.

It is interesting to compare the Kimata figures with the records of other clans at about the same time, which show a difference in priority given to weapon groups. Not all records are as detailed as the Kimata list, and many omit any separate category of foot samurai. Thus the hatamoto of Shimazu Iehisa designated for the siege of Osaka in 1614 consisted of 130 mounted samurai; 456 foot samurai; 200 spearmen; 300 matchlockmen; 200 archers and 261 support troops, plus an unfortunately unspecified number of 'weapon-bearers of the lord's attendants'. Although the omission of the latter figure makes an estimate difficult, the percentage of non-combatant support troops cannot have been much greater than 25, which is less than the Kimata example. The 261 support troops break down as:

- 56 flag-bearers and standard-bearers
- 50 carriers of wooden shields
- 30 carriers of armour chests
- 30 carriers of 100-arrow quiver boxes
- 30 carriers of bullet and powder
- 50 carriers of 1,000 shots of gunpowder each
- 15 grooms with spare horses

Adding a notional 20 weapon-bearers, we reach a grand total of 1,567, more than 17 times the size of Kimata's hatamoto.

The difference in numbers is partly a reflection of the difference in status and wealth of the two men, because Shimazu Iehisa was a daimyō in his own right, whereas Kimata was a vassal of the Ii. But when the comparative proportions are examined, the Kimata contribution at Sekigahara turns out to be the more generous one. Wealth was assessed in koku. One koku was the amount of rice thought necessary to feed

Left: This armour is an example of a comparatively straightforward 'battledress armour' (tosei gusoku) of the Sengoku Period enhanced by the addition of a helmet covered in bear's fur and with a crest in the form of a tengu's pill-box hat. The face mask is typical of the age. The body armour is a dō-maru laced with white kebiki-odoshi (close spaced braid). The sleeves are Bisha-mon-gote style. The haidate (thigh guards) and suneate (shin guards) are both of a simple design. (Courtesy of Christie's)

Right: An armour of nuinobe-dō style, laced in blue sug-ake-odoshi (close-spaced lacing). This is a straightforward 'battledress' armour, of which thousands would have existed during the Sengoku period. The kote (sleeves) are of ikada style. The rus-set iron lacquered finish and dark blue lacing give the whole armour a sombre, workaday appearance. (Cour-tesy of Christie's)

one man for one year, and provided the unit of measurement for the yield of ricefields. Kimata's assessed income in 1600 was 4,000 koku, so he is supplying 90 men at the ratio of 23 men for every 1,000 koku. By comparison, Shimazu Iehisa's force for Osaka was 10,300, of which his hatamoto of 1,567 comprised 15 per cent of the total. Iehisa's income, however, was the princely sum of 770,000 koku in 1614, so he was in fact supplying only 13 men for every 1,000 koku, less than the humble Kimata's earlier contribution to the Tokugawa war effort.

The proportion of troops demanded by a daimyō from assessed wealth varied enormously from year to year, and from campaign to campaign. Various attempts were made to introduce a standard formula, and a contemporary European observer noted that a samurai commander was required to supply 22 men (two mounted men and twenty foot) for each 1,000 koku, but this was by no means a universal rule. In addition, the samurai in question may not have actually supplied for a campaign what the overlord expected.

Returning to the example of Kimata, his hatamoto of 90 men were part of a unit of 800 men, who were in turn just the vanguard of the Ii army, and, looking at the Ii army as a whole, we note that in 1600 Ii Naomasa's income was assessed at 120,000 koku, and he commanded a total force on the Tokugawa side at Sekigahara recorded as 3,600 men, at a ratio of 30 men for every 1,000 koku. By the time of the siege of Osaka in 1614 the Ii wealth had grown to 180,000 koku, from which Ii Naotaka furnished the Tokugawa side with 4,000 men, at the ratio of 22 men per 1,000 koku. Some other contributions on the Tokugawa side are:

Troops supplied per 1,000 koku

Matsudaira Tadaaki	100.0
Ikeda Tadao	79.3
Nanbu Toshinao	30.0
Honda Tadamasa	30.0
Sakai Ietsugu	24.0
Uesugi Kagekatsu	16.6
Date Masamune	16.3
Maeda Toshitsune	8.5

Matsudaira Tadaaki was Tokugawa Ieyasu's grandson, so as a close family member would be expected to supply a large number

Above: Two helmets typical of the Sengoku Period. (Courtesy of Christie's)

Right: Map of central Japan during the Sengoku Period, showing principal battlefields and other places mentioned in the text.

of troops, but the figures give little indication of the actual numbers supplied. The fudai (hereditary vassals) such as Honda, Sakai and Ii, are prominent in their contributions, followed by the tozama (outer lords) who were not hereditary vassals and have submitted to Ieyasu only after Sekigahara. The apparently generous number of troops fielded by the tozama Shimazu has to be taken with a pinch of salt, as they never actually turned up to fight!

Organisation and Communication on the Battlefield

The above analyses thus show that a typical army of the Sengoku Period had certain characteristics which distinguished it from comparable military groupings in previous history. First, its composition was known. It was raised from allies, retainers and family. It could be computed, and was visibly identifiable, being made up from a hierarchy of units, each of whom had a vertically supportive role, and involved distinguishable weapon troops. Second, compared to the

Gempei Wars, the numbers were large. Taking Sekigahara as an example, the Tokugawa contingent, which was the largest part of the total Tokugawa alliance army (known as the Eastern force), consisted of 30,000 troops. There were 3,600 troops supplied by Ii Naomasa, 5,400 supplied by Kuroda Nagamasa, 5,000 supplied by Hosokawa Tadaoki, and most other Eastern armies were about the 3,000 mark. On the Western (Ishida) side we see a larger variation. Ishida Mitsunari fielded 6,000, while two minor daimyō supplied only 600 each. However, the army of Kobayakawa Hideaki, whose defection to the Tokugawa cause was to swing the battle, weighed in at a huge 15,600.

Each of these contingents was assigned its place on the battlefield, and fought independently under the overall command of one supreme general who, in the case of Sekigahara, was Tokugawa Ieyāsu. The greatest disadvantage posed by using separate clan armies was of course the risk of defection, and when Kobayakawa Hideaki turned traitor to the Ishida army, he required only a minimum of reorganisation before he could enter the fray.

The system also had considerable advantages, because the commander would benefit from the fierce loyalty the members of each of these contingents had to one another, with whom they had trained, lived and fought for many years under an identifiable clan standard. Such social homogeneity was regarded as outweighing the lack of similar homogeneity when it came to weaponry. For example, it may have been in the commander's interest to combine, say, three matchlock units from three separate clan armies to make one large firearms squad, but this had to be balanced by the factor of social cohesion. In practical terms it is likely that a compromise was reached whereby three contingents fighting side by side would be required to organise themselves in a similar way, for example with a light screen of archers as skirmishers, and matchlockmen in the front ranks, supported by spearmen. The combined forces would therefore present a homogeneous front to an enemy, without losing any of the clan loyalty.

Naturally it would not be desirable to position clan armies next to one another as one huge front line. Some would be used as second or third contingents to relieve the vanguards, or kept back as the rearguard, and

provinces ————

65

THE LAST DEFENCE OF THE ISHIYAMA HONGAN-JI, 1580

A series of wars against the Buddhist fanatics of the Ikkō-ikki occupied much of the time and energy of Oda Nobunaga. He destroyed their outpost at Nagashima, then turned against their headquarters. This plate is an attempt to reconstruct this final conflict.

As the armies of Oda Nobunaga close in on Ishiyama Hongan-ji, the fortified cathedral of the Ikkō-ikki, the commander Shimotsuma Nakayuki leads his fanatical followers in a last-ditch stand. After eleven years of campaigning the garrison is about to fall. Arrows are protruding from the statue of the fierce god Fudō ('The Immovable One'). Shimotsuma Nakayuki wears the simple suit of armour which is still in the possession of his descendants. His personal sashimono is a giant golden sun on red. The matchlockman next to him proclaims on his flag the conviction that 'He who advances is sure of paradise, but he who retreats will go to hell.' Beside him flies the red banner of one of the Ikkō-ikki contingents from elsewhere in Japan who came to the assistance of the Ishiyama Hongan-ji in its hour of peril. The fall of Ishiyama Hongan-ji, which brought to an end a decade of fighting, was concluded by a peace treaty rather than an assault, and the brave Shimotsuma Nakayuki was spared.

Right: This print by Yoshitoshi depicts the samurai Yamanaka Shika-no-suke Yukimori, the loyal retainer of the Amako family. His helmet bears a crest in the shape of the new moon, a device particularly associated with Yamanaka. His armour is a of a simple mogami-dō style, with flanged upper edges, laced with sugake-odoshi (spaced braid). He carries a cross-bladed spear.

there would always be a central unit of the lord's own hatamoto. In the battle plans of the Sengoku Period each of these positions was designated to one or other single clan unit which, as we have seen, consisted of a mixture of ranks and weapon types. To co-ordinate such a throng required generalship of the highest order, and one factor was common to the age, that the supreme commander did not himself take part in the fighting, as he would have done during the Gempei War, but supervised the entire operation from among his bodyguard set somewhat back from the front line. On occasions this front line could get uncomfortably close, for example during the fourth Battle of Kawanakajima in 1561, when the two generals Uesugi Kenshin and Takeda Shingen fought a brief single combat. But this was the exception rather than the rule, and the hatamoto would sacrifice themselves rather than allow their lord to be harmed.

The key to translating carefully planned strategy into movement on a battlefield, and organising successful action by widely separated and internally heterogeneous clan armies, lay in the speed and bravery of the tsukai-ban, the messengers or aides-de-camp. During a battle these élite mounted warriors, specially chosen from men who were already an élite, would be in constant motion between the commander and the generals of the individual clan armies, taking messages, surveying the situation, reporting back, warning of new developments, and generally providing a high quality battlefield communications system. Other tsukai would perform a similar function in a more restricted area, and could operate on foot. Here their role would be a co-ordinating one of ensuring that the various units moved as one unit, and communicating with the other tsukai. To be of any use in the smoke and confusion of the Sengoku battlefield the tsukai had to be very visible, which they achieved by wearing on the backs of their armour an identifying device, either the balloon-like horō, which was a cloak stretched across a wicker frame, or an outsized version of the samurai's sashimono. Examples included layers of cock's feathers, a large flag with the character go (five) for the Tokugawa, or the appropriate device used by the Takeda which was a busy-looking centipede. Their high visibility, of course, made them the target of every sharp-shooter in the rival

army. The role of the tsukai in controlling a battle is well illustrated on the painted screen depicting the Battle of Nagakute in 1584, which is on display in the Tokugawa Art Museum in Nagoya. The Tokugawa tsukai waits on his horse behind the front line, which, as the flags show, consists of three clan armies standing shoulder to shoulder. Matchlockmen are firing behind a light screen of archers, with spearmen in support.

The Sengoku Battle

To summarise this chapter. The Sengoku battle was fought between alliances of clan armies, deployed according to an agreed battle plan, and co-ordinated through the mobile tsukai-ban. Each clan army was further sub-divided into weapon groups, and co-ordinated through its own band of tsukai. Within each army fought high-ranking mounted samurai spearmen, who also supplied a handful of personal retainers according to their means. Other samurai retainers fought on foot with spears, supported by ashigaru. Specialised corps of highly trained ashigaru were armed with bows, spears or

arquebuses, and all were under the command of officers. A sizeable support unit was included in each army, of which flag-bearers were the most important, and had their own guard. Within each clan army would be a large headquarters unit which formed the lord's bodyguard. This, as shown by the Kimata example, would be an army within an army, reflecting the same overall proportion of rank and weaponry.

In warfare the tsukai-ban or other mounted horsemen, acting as scouts, would locate the enemy, and on drawing close the vanguards would meet. Archers would skirmish, luring the enemy on to the matchlockmen and bowmen who were protected by the spears. When the enemy began to falter the foot samurai would move in with their spears, allowing the cavalry to take the enemy in the flanks. As the vanguard tired, their places would be taken by the second and third units, which might be different clans, and when the enemy broke, reserve units would pursue them. The commander's own clan would be his bodyguard while all this was taking place, with another clan held

Left: The Battle of Nagakute in 1584, showing the co-ordinating function performed by the mounted tsukai-ban of the Tokugawa in the centre of the picture. (Courtesy of the Tokugawa Reimeikai Foundation)

Right: Tokugawa Ieyasu, the ultimate unifier of Japan.

as rearguard to prevent any surprise movements, or to cover lines of withdrawal.

Such careful strategic planning, with the co-operation between separate clan armies facilitated by a skilled battlefield communication system, enabled the successful commander to control synchronised movement by units who were physically separated. That, at any rate, was the theory; an ideal somewhat different from the Gempei War picture of arrow duels and single combat, but every bit as romantic in its own variation on the perfect act of samurai endeavour. Yet despite the increase in numbers and the development in organisation and weaponry, there is a remarkable current of consistency running through samurai warfare. The basic fighting unit is still the small, mutually supporting group, with the same tension between the needs of the group and the demand for individual glory. There is also the same danger that two armies will be so similar that stalemate will ensue, a situation that can only be resolved, as during the Gempei Wars, by the element of ground, defence or surprise.

The Sengoku battle was, however, a much larger animal than its earlier predecessors, and for such a system to work there had to be organisation. Each man, in every troop, had to understand exactly what his functions and responsibilities were. The chain of command had to be linked by the finest of battlefield communication systems, so that each man knew what his role was in the current endeavour. The Sengoku daimyō possessed sufficient resources to support such a model, to supply and train their armies and to ensure their continuing loyalty. Most importantly, they possessed sufficient wealth in the form of rice lands to allow their fighting men to be virtually professional soldiers, with no part-time requirements for agricultural work. This was the basis of the system which the ultimately successful Tokugawa family formalised as the rigid class hierarchy of samurai, farmer, merchant and others, with no social mobility between them. The distinction between samurai and the rest of Japanese society was therefore the final legacy of the Sengoku battlefield, the high-water mark of samurai warfare.

Chapter 6

SPECIALISED UNITS IN THE SENGOKU ARMY

The tsukai-ban were the only specialist arm within a clan army to be drawn from the samurai ranks. The use of ashigaru in their vital supportive role as warrior attendants, flag-bearers and baggage-carriers has already been noted, but within each clan army would be found a varying percentage of three key specialised units of ashigaru: archers, spearmen and matchlockmen, plus, in later years, certain specialists in artillery. This chapter will examine the precise role of each of these arms.

Archers and Spearmen

It is difficult to conclude from muster records which of the three ashigaru specialities was the most highly valued, as numbers vary, and may indicate no more than shortage of supply of certain weapons. In 1592 the Shimazu clan army which went to Korea included 1,500 archers, 1,500 matchlockmen and 300 spearmen. In the same year the hatamoto of Date Masamune included 50 archers, 100 matchlockmen and 100 spearmen. In 1600 the same Date family supplied the Tokugawa with a clan army of 3,000, made up of 420 mounted samurai, 200 archers, 1,200 matchlockmen, 850 spearmen and 330 support troops.

Among the missile troops, archers had the longest tradition, and with the shift from mounted samurai archer to mounted samurai spearmen lower-ranked troops were given the opportunity to develop skill with the bow. The ashigaru archers were highly trained sharpshooters, and were often employed as skirmishers. In addition they could form lines of missile troops along with the matchlockmen, supplied with a large number of arrows carried in 100-arrow box quivers. These were often carried by an attendant. Archers sometimes appear to be regarded as the least important of the three arms, and in the 1575 Uesugi muster rolls they are included within the 'other troops' category (total 1,018), beside 3,609 spearmen, 321 matchlockmen and 566 mounted samurai.

The second force, that of the spearmen, has also often been given cursory treatment, their role being dismissed when compared to the matchlockmen. Their spears have been regarded as comparatively short weapons, virtually identical with those carried by the samurai. However, recent research has shown that they were frequently regarded as more important than matchlockmen. Oda Nobunaga, who was probably the first to introduce disciplined ashigaru spear units, had a contingent that made up 27 per cent of

Left: Sasa Narimasa appears on this print by Kuniyoshi, but his name is written as 'Sada Arimasa'. This was a curious device sometimes found on prints whereby the artist circumvented the ban imposed by the Tokugawa Shōgunate against representing historical personages. He wears a sashimono banner typical of the Sengoku Period, bearing a design of a black oni (demon). He carries a whip in his right hand, ready to urge his horse down the snow-covered slopes towards his enemy Hideyoshi in 1588.

his fighting force, compared to 13.5 per cent for matchlocks. In 1575 the Uesugi had ten spearmen for every matchlockman.

New research has also revealed that the typical Sengoku ashigaru spearmen carried a weapon that was very long, and more akin to a pike, thus calling into question the whole concept of how this vital arm was used. The early spears were the same as samurai ones, but there is a noticeable lengthening of the shaft of the ashigaru weapon as the century progresses, producing the nagae-yari (long-shafted spear). The shaft was of composite construction, with a core of hardwood such as oak, surrounded by laminations of bamboo. The whole shaft was lacquered to weather-proof it. As with bows and matchlocks, considerable training was needed in the use of such a long weapon, making the spearmen every bit as specialised a weapon unit as their comrades. The use of polearms by mounted samurai, foot samurai and ashigaru thus made spears of all lengths the most commonly seen weapon on the battlefield, and by about 1570 the breakdown of weaponry within the Hōjō armies included between one-third and a half of all men (samurai and

ashigaru) armed with spears. Within the Takeda clan the proportion was between one half and two-thirds. For the Uesugi, in the figures quoted above for 1575, the proportion is two-thirds. Foot samurai, however, are not mentioned as a separate category, but are included within the mounted samurai numbers.

The total length of nagae-yari differed from clan to clan according to the general's preference, the length of shaft being usually about 3 ken. At the start of the Sengoku Period one ken was equivalent to 1.6 metres (the dimensions changed later to 1.8 metres), so the length of the spear shaft would have been 4.8 metres. There was more variation in the length of the samurai's mochi-yari, as noted in the previous chapter. The Takeda used a nagae-yari shaft of 3 ken, while their mochi-yari, including blade, were 2½ ken. Uesugi Kenshin used a shaft of 2½ ken for his nagae-yari, while his successor Kagekatsu (1555–1623) used 3 ken at about the time of Sekigahara, as did Toyotomi Hideyoshi. The Tokugawa also used a 3 ken shaft for nagae-yari, but favoured a somewhat shorter mochi-yari at between 2 and 2½ ken in total.

Left: Two spears, their blades in scabbards, hang from the ceiling in an old samurai's house near Sasebo.

Left: The troops of Oda Nobunaga confirm the superiority of their extra-long spears in a mock battle with troops furnished for demonstration purposes by Toyotomi Hideyoshi.

The Date family liked a 3 ken shaft lacquered red. The longest spears of all were used by Oda Nobunaga, with a giant 3½ ken (5.6 metres) shaft. This would appear to be a development Nobunaga adopted quite early in his career, because there is a reference in the Shinchōkōki dated April 1553 to '500 3½ ken long spears'.

Because of their size the nagae-yari had the potential to cause as much trouble for friend as for foe if their use was not coordinated properly, and there is ample evidence from contemporary accounts that a form of 'pike-drill' evolved during the Age of War. The spear units were under the command of an ashigaru-taishō, who would arrange the men in ranks each about one man apart. The blades would be unsheathed, and the scabbards placed through the belt. If a cavalry attack was expected the spearmen would kneel, with their spears lying on the ground. As the horsemen approached they would rise up, ordering their ranks to provide an even line of blades.

When advancing to an enemy the blades would again be aligned, and the ranks would move forward slowly, keeping an even rhythm. An example of such a movement is included in the chronicle Ou Eikei Gunki:

Iyo Chōza'emonjō Sadahira and Ichikuri Heibū Shōrin with 300 men, plus the forces under Yoshida Magoichi and Nishin Shūri Ryōshun and Magosaburō of the same family with 500 men, arranged their spearblades in an even line and went to fight against the Yuzawa side.

The Introduction of Firearms

Several references have already been made to the use of matchlock muskets, otherwise known as arquebuses, in samurai warfare. From very early in their introduction they were used as ashigaru weapons, and eventually produced major changes in warfare, so that it became more of a process of using professional soldiers, most of whom, including the lower ranks, were on retained service, dressed uniformly, and were well trained. The usual conclusion is to see the introduction of firearms as the cause, and the change in warfare as the result, of a single process.

It may be that guns had been known about for many years prior to their intro-duction by the Portuguese in 1542. But if so these would have been unsophisticated Chinese weapons, and could not have had the sensational impact upon Japan that the handful of Portuguese arquebuses produced. The island on which the Portuguese landed, Tanegashima, was owned by the Shimazu clan, and it was to Shimazu Takahisa that the honour went of conducting the first battle in Japanese history at which firearms were used. This was in his attack on the fortress of Kajiki, in Osumi province, in 1549. He was one of several warlords to appreciate the potential shown by these new weapons, and local swordsmiths, who were already renowned for their metal-working skills, applied themselves to learning the necessary techniques, first to copy the arquebuses, and then to mass-produce them. Connections with Portuguese traders also proved very important, and it is no coincidence that the first Christian converts among the samurai class became regular users of arquebuses. 'Don Juan' Ichibu Kageyu, a vassal of the Matsuura daimyō of Hirado, is a case in point. This staunch Christian samurai made good use of firearms at the Battle of Aikō no Ura in 1563, and later used them against pirates who had come to plunder his island of Ikitsuki. Two of the three pirate ships were sunk, and when Ichibu came to investigate the corpses, all had died from bullet wounds rather than from arrows.

The Portuguese arquebus was a simple, but well-designed weapon. Unlike the heavier type of muskets, which required a rest, the arquebus could be fired from the shoulder, with support needed only for the heavier calibre versions developed later by the Japanese, which are usually known as 'wall guns' or 'hand cannon'. In a normal arquebus an iron barrel fitted neatly into a wooden stock, to the right of which was a brass serpentine linked to a spring, which dropped the serpentine when the trigger was pulled. The serpentine contained the end of a glowing and smouldering match, the rest of which was wrapped around the stock of the gun, or wound around the gunner's arm. Arquebuses are therefore often called simply 'matchlocks'. As a precaution against premature ignition the pan, into which the fine, priming gunpowder had been carefully introduced, was closed by a brass sliding cover, which was swung back at the last moment. The gun produced quite a recoil, and a lot of smoke, as shown in the annual festival at Nagashino where reproduction matchlocks are fired. As skills developed, cartridges were introduced, thus speeding up the process of loading.

One technical problem the Japanese faced was how to close the end of the barrel where it fitted into the stock. According to legend, one blacksmith of the Shimazu exchanged his daughter for a series of lessons! A Portuguese adventurer subsequently wrote that within two or three years the Japanese had succeeded in making several hundred guns, and by the 1550s they were regularly seen in action in battle. The best gunsmiths formed schools to pass on the tradition, such as those at Kunitomo and Sakai, and were never short of customers. In 1549 Oda Nobunaga placed an order for 500 arquebuses with the gunsmiths of Kunitomo. In 1555 Takeda Shingen used 300 in an attack on a castle owned by Uesugi Kenshin, and was so impressed that he placed 500 arque-

buses in one of his own castles. By 1569 he had such faith in firearms that he could write to his retainers:

Hereafter guns will be the most important. Therefore decrease the number of spears and have your most capable men carry guns. Furthermore, when you assemble your soldiers, test their marksmanship and order that the selection be carried out in accordance with the results.

This letter may be evidence of over-enthusiasm, because guns were never as plentiful as spears, nor as readily available, yet within the space of a few years arquebuses were being produced to quality standards that exceeded those originally brought from Europe. One simple but fundamental development which occurred quite early on in Japanese arquebus production was the standardisation of the bore. In Europe, where no form of standardisation was carried out,

Below: The final processes involved in firing an arquebus, from right to left: ramming the ball, preparing the powder for the pan; priming the pan; cocking the serpentine; firing.

Right: Inaue Masa-tada, a retainer of Uesugi Kenshin, is shown in this print by Kuniyoshi in the act of firing a large-calibre matchlock gun. His armour is a kebiki-laced dō-maru, and his sashimono flag bears the device of a death's head.

practically every gun needed its own bullet mould. In Japan bores were standardised to a handful of sizes. Standard bores meant standard sized bullets, which could be carried in bulk for an arquebus corps, a small, but significant improvement in production and use.

The efficiency and accuracy of the matchlock musket have recently been assessed in a series of practical experiments carried out in Japan, using Japanese arquebuses made at the beginning of the Edo Period. The first test was an assessment of the gun's range. Five bullets, each of 8mm calibre, were fired at a target in the shape of an armoured samurai from distances of 30 metres and 50 metres respectively by an experienced matchlock user. At 30 metres each of the five bullets hit the target area of the chest, but only one out of the five struck the chest area at 50 metres. At the Battle of Nagashino in 1575 the guns began firing at a range of about 50 metres, but as they were firing at mounted men they had a much larger effective target area, and to unhorse a samurai and

The stone-base design also had the advantage of providing the best resistance to earthquakes, which have always been a problem in Japan. The great disadvantage, of course, was that a wall that slopes outwards is ideally situated for attackers to climb, but once again Japanese ingenuity came to the fore, and trap doors similar to European machicolations were built into the towers, which later were also made to slightly overhang the stone bases. Kumamoto castle in Kyushu is the best example of this. Arrows could therefore be fired down on to the heads of attackers, in addition to allowing the launching of anything else that the defenders could usefully lob in their direction! Woodblock prints show the simple use of rocks as projectiles, which would bounce off the curved stone walls and create havoc. The defenders would be standing on an ishi uchi tana. Huge logs, held up by ropes until required, could also be employed in this fashion. Gatehouses, keeps and corner towers were also built with stone bases, and gradually the openwork towers seen at Sakurai gave way to stronger yet more graceful multi-storey buildings with curved and tiled roofs that are found in surviving examples of castle construction.

The progress of an attacker could further be hindered by the use of caltrops, which we noted above during the Heian Period, the metal spikes so arranged that they always landed with one spike pointing upwards. The samurai invariably wore straw sandals, so this was quite effective. Fences of stakes would also be built at the bottom of dry moats to slow down attackers and thereby provide better targets for sharpshooters from

THREE GENERALS OF TOYOTOMI HIDEYOSHI DURING THE KYUSHU CAMPAIGN, 1587

Toyotomi Hideyoshi's reduction of Japan's southern island of Kyushu required the largest military operation yet seen in samurai warfare. H_ _ _ supported by several outstanding generals, three of _ _ _ _ _ conferring in camp, while ashigaru be_ _ _ _ _ _ _nners. On the left is Ishida N_ _ attention throug_ _ ined to be the lo_ _ His armour is v_ black horse hai_ unusual breast_ a blue utility _ a flag with a _ nobori flags _ and Takayar_ jirushi with Hideyoshi'_

The arm_ example c_ could be _ hisa's da_ ornamer_ fered d_ Hetsug_ acter n_

The one o_ most_ Shiz_ the _ the _ bl_ H_ n_

ack on Oiwa Shizu-paign of ving . and kmen.

ers, ranging from solid constructions with roofs, to mobile ones on huge wooden wheels. One variety, credited to Takeda Shingen's strategist, Yamamoto Kansuke, consisted of a box on a pulley. The scout would be hauled up to make his observations, and then hauled down as soon as the defenders got his range. The Japanese also invented two varieties of mobile shield. Both were on a prism-shaped framework on wooden wheels. One was of solid planks, the other of bundles of green bamboo, which could absorb shots. Each would have weapon slits cut through and would be wheeled up to the castle to provide cover for two or three sharpshooters. Rice straw bundles and sandbags were also used for defensive cover. But throughout samurai history these were only means to an end, the end being that of bringing brave samurai warriors face to face on the castle walls. As late as 1877, during the Satsuma Rebellion, we read of the traditionalist rebels fighting sword in hand against the new conscripts of the Imperial army armed with their European rifles, as they struggled for control of the walls of Kumamoto castle.

Left: In the little town of Kotari, midway between Osaka and Kyōto, lie the reconstructed outer walls of Shōryūji castle, providing an excellent example of defensive works during the mid-Sengoku Period. The outer defence is a narrow moat, with a grassy bank leading up to low stone walls, on which are raised walls of wood and plaster about 5 metres high in all. A small corner tower contains a projecting trap door. The castle probably looked very much like this during the Battle of Yamazaki in 1582, which was fought nearby.

Left: A sturdy stone bridge crossing the moat to a simple but solidly reinforced side gate to Fukue castle, on the Gotō island group. The walls are of stone, and weathered with age. The plaster upper sections have square apertures for archery and triangular ones for guns.

Above: At Hikone castle this high wooden bridge crosses a dry moat to the Tenpinyagura turret, which contains the last but one gateway before the keep. This fine example of later Sengoku military architecture featured in the film 'Shōgun'.

Below: The defenders of Yakiyama castle loosen the planks of the bridge, and the attackers fall to their deaths.

okegawa-dō style, lacquered black with a solid breastplate, and have the Matsuura mon of three stars lacquered on the front in gold.

The Matsuura Kakemono

In the earlier description of the hatamoto of Kimata Morikatsu and Shimazu Iehisa the figures for their armies were analysed in terms of function and rank. It is possible to do the same for the Matsuura, and the Matsuura data actually allows us to go further and see how the ranks and groups were deployed on the battlefield. The source for this is the large kakemono (hanging scroll) displayed in the Matsuura Historical

Museum in Hirado. As the scroll shows the Matsuura army prepared for battle rather than in a procession or engaged in fighting it is almost unique as a historical record of this aspect of samurai warfare.

The background to its commission is as follows. The 29th daimyō of the Hirado han (fief), a second Matsuura Shigenobu (1637–89) was on intimate terms with the great strategist Yamaga Sokō (1622–85), and organised the Matsuura army according to Yamaga's recommendations. His views with regard to army organisation are illustrated on the scroll as they were to be seen in a practical demonstration in the year 1796, when they were under the command of the enthu-

Below left: The front ranks of the Matsuura army, showing matchlockmen, archers and officers.

Below: The second and third ranks of the Matsuura army: spearmen and samurai.

siastic 34th daimyō, Matsuura Seizan Kiyoshi (1775–1806). The scroll therefore represents the Matsuura army as it would have appeared in about 1650, the time of the publication of O-uma jirushi. This is also the time that saw the issue of the final schedule of the Shōgun's requirements for the supply of men and equipment among the Tokugawa's own retainers, according to income. Making allowances for the progressive reduction in numbers included in the revisions published in 1616 and 1633, and then finally in 1649, and applying them to a daimyō, the Matsuura kakemono may be used as the basis for visualising the Matsuura army at the end of the Sengoku Period.

Below: The commander, Matsuura Seizan Kiyoshi, indicated by the pointer, with his bodyguard around him.

Taking the layout as a whole, Sōko's ideas with regard to battle formations were nothing revolutionary, and the positions adopted by Matsuura Kiyoshi are very similar to several standard battle formations recommended by military thinkers during the Sengoku Period. Spearmen protect matchlockmen to front, flanks and rear, and the samurai form a third rank, while the general is surrounded by a half-circle of retainers, with flags and drum to hand. The first point of comparison between the figures on the scroll and the data for the Korean War is the vast difference in numbers. Shigenobu took 3,000 men to Korea, while the scroll shows only 650, of whom 238 can be identified as support troops. This figure (37 per cent of the total) is reached after including within the fighting men all the flag-bearers and drummers. There is, however, no pack train. The overall figures are also somewhat approximate, as I tend to count a different number every time I analyse the scroll! The number no doubt reflects the changed circumstances between peace and war. However, as studies of other clan armies have shown, the proportion of troop functions within an army tended to remain fairly constant, so it is possible to take the proportions on the scroll as evidence of the make-up of the Matsuura's Sengoku army. This is supported by the fact that in most cases the heraldry of the various corps match up with the description of the Namwön action and the later list. The detailed breakdown is:

The Commander's Retinue

The lord, Matsuura Seizan Kiyoshi	1
Foot samurai, varied armour, red/ white sashimono	20
Foot samurai, red striped armour, no sashimono	28
Foot samurai, red disc on armour, no sashimono	20
The lord's spearmen	26
Non-samurai attendants to the lord	24
Mounted samurai	20
Attendants to the mounted samurai	160
Foot samurai, varied armour, black/white sashimono	50
Attendants to the above samurai	54

Specialised ashigaru

Matchlockmen	104
Archers	32

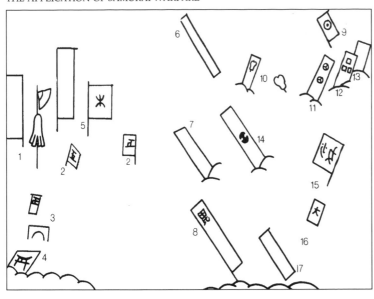

ANEGAWA SCREEN

In its way, the painted screen of the Battle of Anegawa represents an ideal of samurai warfare comparable to the written
accounts of early battles in the gunkimono. The fighting shown
on the screen is conducted entirely by samurai. Almost all the
figures are either named individual generals, or their most
senior retainers. There are no ranks of ashigaru spearmen or
matchlockmen, the only role for lower-ranking troops shown
on the screen being that of the bearers of the samurai's personal banner, which indicated his physical location in battle.
Here the link between a samurai and his attendant is shown
very clearly.

The screen is none the less very important as a source for the
heraldry of the contending forces. Almost all the commanders
listed in the text are shown on the screen, together with many
of the retainers who made a name for themselves that day,
such as Makara.

Left Panels

1. Tokugawa Ieyasu, the commander of the Tokugawa army. He sits under his golden fan standard. His Jōdo banner
   is shown as two separate flags. The Tokugawa mon appears on two white hata-jirushi.
2. Three foot samurai who are members of Ieyasu's tsukai-ban, as indicated by the sashimono.
3. The flag, with a wheel device, of Sakakibara Yasumasa (1548–1606), one of Ieyasu's generals.
4. The flag of General Torii Mototada (1539–1600), with a torii gate on it.
5. Okubo Tadayo (1531–93), one of Ieyasu's most loyal generals. His attendant holds his black personal banner. His
   own sashimono is a three-dimensional golden butterfly.
6. A warrior monk of the Heisen-ji temple, named Sairin Bōzu, who is fighting for the Asakura. He wears a monk's
   cowl, and his attendant holds a banner with a Buddhist prayer on it.
7. Ikeda Nobuteru (1536–84), who led 3,000 men in Nobunaga's army.
8. Uwozumi Kageyuki, a retainer of the Asakura, who was killed during the Battle of the Anegawa. His red banner
   bears the character 'bi', which indicates the deity Bishamonten.
9. The coin flag indicates the presence of Sengoku Hidehisa (1551–1614), of the Oda army.

10. The fan design indicates Okudaira Sadayoshi, a Mikawa samurai whose son Nobumasa was to achieve fame at the siege of Nagashino. Behind it is a gourd-shaped flag, and to the right the golden gourd standard, both belonging to Toyotomi Hideyoshi.

11. The 'propeller' is the badge of Yamauchi Kazutoyo (1546–1605), serving Nobunaga.

12. Suganuma Sadamitsu (1542–1604), of the Tokugawa force.

13. Part of the flag of Shitara Sadamichi, another Tokugawa retainer, can be seen behind '12'.

14. Matsudaira Shigekatsu (1548–1620), one of seventeen named samurai of the Matsudaira (Ieyasu's own family) present at Anegawa.

15. The large blue banner, bearing the character myō (mystery) identifies Watanabe Hanzō Moritsuna, 'Devil Hanzō', one of Ieyasu's celebrated generals. His own sashimono is a red bucket!

16. Okubo Tadachika (1553–1628), son of Tadayo, whose attendant carries a similar black banner. His sashimono is also a butterfly.

17. Maeba Shinhachirō, one of the commanders of the Asakura army, killed at Anegawa together with his brother Shintarō.

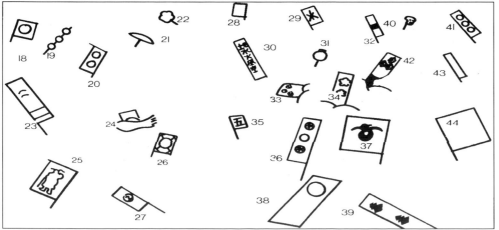

ANEGAWA SCREEN: RIGHT PANELS

18. Matsudaira Ietada (1547–82).

19. The three balls are the sashimono of Takigawa Kazumasu, who served Oda Nobunaga.

20. Honda Tadakatsu (1548–1610), another Tokugawa loyalist.

21. One of the shichi hon yari (seven spears) of Anegawa, the title given to the seven most valiant warriors in the Tokugawa army at Anegawa. This one has a sashimono of an enormous red umbrella!

22. Judging by the mon, this is probably a standard of Oda Nobunaga.

23. Matsudaira Nobukazu (1548–1632), Ieyasu's uncle, whose badge was two red fans.

24. Matsudaira Koretada (1537–75), who used the Tokugawa mon.

25. Maeda Toshiie (1538–99) with his instantly recognisable banner depicting Shōki the Demon-Queller. His sashimono is a golden fan, and his helmet badge is one golden antler.

26. Makara Jūrōzaemon, whose exploits at the Anegawa earned him the respect of both sides. He is wielding his nodachi, while his attendant lifts high his personal banner of two white zig-zags on blue. His sashimono is unusual. It is supposed to represent a gong, suspended at four corners, symbolic in Buddhism of the overcoming of earthly passions.

27. The bird device of Gamō Ujisato (1557–96), of the Oda force.

28. Another of the shichi hon yari, with a blue flag.

29. This is probably Mizuno Tadashige (1541–1600), Ieyasu's cousin.

30. A third shichi hon yari, named as Monna Sakon'emon. His sashimono bears the names of the five elements according to Chinese lore: earth, water, fire, wind and air.

31. A fourth shichi hon yari, named as Yoshihara Matabei, with a sashimono of a red lantern.

32. Another shichi hon yari with a black and white flag.

33. The white nobori flag lying horizontally is a banner of the Asakura. The red design is the Asakura mon, which is like three of Oda Nobunaga's mon, but slightly 'squashed'.

34. The red nobori bears the mon of Oda Nobunaga.

35. One of Ieyasu's tsukai-ban, going about his business.

36. The prominent white nobori indicates Ishikawa Kazumasa, who led 1,000 men in the Tokugawa army. The golden flower standard is probably his also.

37. Shibata Katsuie (1530–83) commanded 3,000 men at the Battle of Anegawa in the Oda army. His personal banner is a large red flag with a design of a plover.

38. The rising sun flag belongs to Kurosaka Kagenori, retainer of the Asakura, killed at the Battle of Anegawa.

39. The deathblow is delivered by Ogasawara Nagatada, who led 1,000 men in the Tokugawa army. His white nobori appears behind him on the next panel.

40. Sixth of the shichi hon yari, Fushiki Kyūnai has a sashimono of a three-dimensional skull.

41. The three suns on white of Sakai Tadatsugu (1527–96), one of Ieyasu's Shi-tennō (four faithful retainers). The others were Honda Tadakatsu, Ii Naomasa and Sakakibara Yasumasa.

42. A standard-bearer with the banner of Asai Nagamasa, in black on white.

43. Last of the shichi hon yari. He is named as Date Yōhei, and wears a sashimono with the 'earth, fire, water, wind, air' slogan on red.

44. A certain Ryūmōnji Hyōgo no suke advances to the assistance of the Asakura as their defences collapse. He may have been a warrior monk. His large banner bears invocations of three Shintō gods: Hachiman Dai Bosatsu (the god of war); Amaterasu Kōtai Jingu (the name of the shrine of the sun-goddess); Kasuga Daimyōjin (the god enshrined at the Kasuga shrine in Nara).

THE DEFENCE OF UEDA CASTLE BY THE SANADA FAMILY IN 1600

In 1600, during the campaign that ended with the Battle of Sekigahara, an army commanded by Tokugawa Hidetada set out from Edo along the Nakasendō, the road that ran through the central mountains of Japan, with the intention of joining his father Tokugawa Ieyasu. But on the way Hidetada began to lay siege to the castle of Ueda, held by the father and son team of Sanada Masayuki and Sanada Yukimura. So desperately was their castle defended that Tokugawa Hidetada abandoned the siege, which had so delayed him that he missed the Battle of Sekigahara, an omission that could have had very serious consequences had the victory not already been secured by the treachery of Kobayakawa.

Sanada Masayuki is seen directing ashigaru to their posts as the Tokugawa army (visible through the trapdoor) advance to the walls. He is wearing an armour that is still preserved in Ueda. It is a very straightforward 'battledress', clearly designed for action rather than for show, and consisting of an okegawa-dō with kebiki-style yellow laced kusazuri. The haidate and kote are all 'standard issue' in black lacquer, the only addition the commander has allowed himself being the enormous silver helmet badge. Unusually for one of samurai rank, the armour bears one of the Sanada mon in silver on its breastplate.

Behind Masayuki stands a teppō ko gashira (firearms lieutenant) the quality of whose armour is midway between that of his lord and his fellow ashigaru. He gesticulates with a red-lacquered bamboo 'swagger stick' inside which is a spare ramrod, a great help should any of the gunners be unfortunate enough to break his own. The heraldic device of a ladder is repeated on front and rear of the armour of his ashigaru. One by one they reach for their matchlock muskets from the racks on the walls. Coils of fuse are conveniently located above the gun racks. As they are operating within the close confines of a castle they do not wear sashimono flags on their backs, nor do they carry ration bags. Pouches for bullets and powder are slung from their belts. Behind them an archer takes a hasty pot-shot out of a trapdoor at the attackers below.

Shigenari, who is probably the one wearing the large white horo on his back, and the samurai with black flags under Gotō Mototsugu. When the moment was right they made a sudden charge. The Satake men were forced to withdraw, and there were many casualties among Satake's vanguard, and the main body of the Satake army only succeeded in holding on to Imafuku after themselves receiving reinforcements from Uesugi Kagekatsu.

Uesugi Kagekatsu's army of 5,000 had in fact already been engaged in battle with 2,000 Osaka troops across the river at a place called Shigeno. Reinforcements arrived from Niwa Nagashige and Horio Tadatoki, who were well supported by matchlock musketeers. Ieyasu ordered Horio to take over from Uesugi to let him rest, which received the harsh retort that the Uesugi samurai had the tradition of never retiring once a fight had started.

Three days later, on the 29th, two separate naval operations took place. Following a reconnaissance of the area to the west of the castle beside the Kizu river, Ieyasu ordered Ishikawa Tadafusa to capture the fort that controlled this section. Ishikawa mounted an elaborate amphibious operation, co-ordinating a crossing by his army of 2,300 from the west, with an attack from the east and south by Hachisuka Yoshishige, each facilitated by crossing waterways in boats. The fort succumbed rapidly.

Meanwhile, at nearby Toda-Fukushima, the guard ships of the Tokugawa, under the overall command of Kuki Moritaka (son of the late admiral Yoshitaka), took advantage of a heavy rain storm to attack Ono Harunaga. The Eastern ships had 1,600 men on board against Ono's 800, and their victory prevented any support being given to the other operation under Ishikawa.

The final major action of the Winter Campaign was the attack on the Sanada barbican on 4 December. The screen shows the attack approaching, led by samurai whose banners identify them as the troops of Matsudaira Tadanao (1595–1650), grandson of Tokugawa Ieyasu. They are followed close behind by the Ii samurai, who assaulted the wall further along and managed to scale the ramparts until a counter-attack by Kimura Shigenari drove them back. In all, 10,000 Eastern troops attacked the barbican, but were held off by Sanada's 7,000. Other skirmishes took place when the defenders sallied out to surprise the Tokugawa army. On the screen we see the night attack of 17 December launched out of the castle's eastern walls across the Honmachi bridge, illuminated by lanterns. This was a minor victory for the Osaka army, as their force of 150 men under Hanawa Naoyuki defeated the Tokugawa troops in the siege lines.

Apart from these two reverses the operations of the Winter Campaign had all gone the Easterners' way. The outlying forts and the waterways were all secure, but the defence of the Sanada barbican had shown

Left: A section from the painted screen depicting the Winter Campaign of Osaka, showing the Battle of Imafuku on 26 November 1614. Satake Yoshinobu's forces of 1,500, shown by the mon of a fan on their flags, charge into the troops of Gotō Mototsugu (black flags) and Kimura Shigenari (red flags).

Above: The 7,000 strong force of Nabeshima Katsushige (1580–1657) are galvanised into action by a night attack across the river from Osaka castle. Two ashigaru light fires. Other ashigaru matchlockmen fire into the castle from behind the protection of bundles of bamboo built up on an earthen mound, or rice bales stuffed with sand.

Below: The complex details of the siege lines to the north of Osaka castle are revealed here in this section from the 'Winter Campaign' screen. At the top the troops of Arima Toyouji (800 men) establish a position on the remains of the bridge to the castle using sandbags. The colours used on the screen are somewhat arbitrary, and were in fact black and white rather than black and pink. To the right the soldiers of Mōri Hidenari, with red and white flags, establish another defensive position in front of wooden shields. Below them can be seen the flags of Katō Akinari (800 men).

Left: The attack on the Sanada barbican is led by the samurai of Matsudaira Tadanao (1595–1650), whose banners are white with a black 'y'-shaped device. He led 10,000 men at Osaka. He is followed into the attack by the Ii, in their characteristic red armour. The Sanada barbican is shown as a fortified palisade, with two levels for fighting men. The upper levels have wooden inner parapets. Here ashigaru in simple armour crouch down with guns. Note the mon on the back of their armour.

135

Campaign Hideyori was able to cram within its walls more troops than in the previous year. It was also the Osaka army that first took the offensive, ambushing various contingents of the Tokugawa army while they were still on their way. These actions included one operation many miles from Osaka, when Ono Harunaga, Hanawa Naoyuki and Okabe Noritsuna attempted to capture the castle of Wakayama in Kii province. The castle was owned by Asano Nagaakira, most of whose troops had already moved up to the Osaka siege lines. The Western force numbered 3,000 men. Realising that their enemies were perilously far from support, the castle garrison of 5,000 men boldly moved out to meet them in battle at Kashii. Hanawa and Okabe were both killed in the vanguard, forcing Ono to withdraw to the safety of the Osaka garrison.

The decision facing Toyotomi Hideyori was whether or not to risk a long blockade, which would now have the added threat of a full-scale assault against the weakened castle. A council of war was held on 2 June 1615, and it was resolved that the Osaka troops would take the fight to the enemy. A series of battles took place to the south of the castle on the 6th, reaching a climax with the Battle of Tennōji on the 7th, around the area now occupied by Tennōji station. Like the Winter Campaign, a meticulously detailed painted screen has preserved a pictorial record of the Battle of Tennōji and its disastrous aftermath.

The action began on 6 June with an engagement known as the Battle of Dōmyōji, fought to the south-east of the castle along the road to Nara. The objective of the Western Army was to control this area ready for their major assault. They proved to be vastly outnumbered, as Gotō Mototsugu's 6,400 men found themselves opposed by major troop concentrations of 23,000 under Date Masamune and others. Gotō quickly abandoned the operation and pulled back, rallying his men to the nearby high ground of Komatsuyama, helped by dense fog. Reinforcements sent to them by the Osaka garrison found it difficult to make contact in the fog, and Gotō Mototsugu, one of the ablest generals on the Osaka side, was killed in action. The Eastern army pressed on across the Yamato river, where

Below: Sanada Yukimura, whose army is on the left, fights Honda Tadatomo.

they met a second wave from the castle numbering 12,000. Matsudaira Tadaaki and Mizuno Katsushige attacked Mōri Katsunaga, while to the south Date Masamune's army engaged Sanada Yukimura. Eventually all armies disengaged after heavy casualties, with no victory recognised by either side.

That same day two further engagements took place about 8 kilometres to the north at Hachio and Wakae. This was a low-lying and damp area where the rivers Nagase and Tamagushi flowed. Here the 5,300 men of Chōsokabe Morichika's Western army took on and defeated Tōdō Takatora's 5,000 men. The reverse happened at nearby Wakae. Here the Westerners had 4,700 men under the enthusiastic Kimura Shigenari, who received a spirited charge from Ii Naotaka. This is the attack depicted on the painted screen in Hikone castle. In this assault Kimurai Shigenari was killed, and when his head was presented to Ieyasu it was noted that he had perfumed the inside of his helmet so as to make it a more attractive trophy. On this one day the Western army had lost two of its finest men.

The following day the Osaka garrison committed everything into one final battle. The Toyotomi plan was that Sanada Yukimura and Ono Harunaga would deliver a frontal assault on the Tokugawa main body, who would be held in combat while Akashi Morishige swept round to deliver an attack from the rear. When all the Tokugawa troops were engaged Hideyori would lead the garrison out of the castle, bearing aloft the golden gourd standard of his late father.

The Tokugawa army had occupied positions some distance from the remaining walls, with Honda Tadatomo in the vanguard, Date Masamune on the left flank, and Ii Naotaka and Maeda Toshitsune on the right. The rearguard was provided by Asano Nagaakira, whose troops touched the sea coast. The distance between the armies gave the Osaka contingent ample opportunity for careful grouping and timing to coincide with Akashi's sweep round. But controlled tactical manoeuvres were not to the liking of rōnin, and as soon as Mōri Katsunaga's men came within sight of the Tokugawa vanguard they opened up on them with their arquebuses. Fearful that his careful plans would be ruined by this impetuosity, Sanada ordered them to cease firing, but they only redoubled their efforts. Mōri consulted Sanada who

agreed that the best way of resolving the difficulty was for an immediate full-scale attack, so as Mōri Katsunaga led his men forward in a charge which broke through into the Tokugawa main body, Sanada Yukimura assaulted the Tokugawa left flank, and sent a messenger back to the castle with a request for Toyotomi Hideyori to join the battle at once.

Here chance was on his side, because even though his men under Akashi were far from able to deliver the rear attack, certain of the Tokugawa army appeared to be doing it for them. That at any rate was the conclusion drawn by many of the Tokugawa main body who saw their rearguard under Asano wheel towards them. Cries of 'Treachery!' went up from many throats, who feared that Asano had turned against them. In fact he had not, but Tokugawa Ieyasu himself was forced to join his men in the thick of the fighting to steady their nerves. Here, according to tradition, Sanada Yukimura engaged him in a very brief single combat, and wounded him in the kidneys with his spear blade.

It was Honda Tadatomo who saved the day. He led his troops in a charge against Sanada Yukimura. Sanada was driven back, and, physically exhausted, collapsed on a camp stool. A certain samurai recognised him and made a challenge, but Sanada was too tired to reply, so the man sliced off his head. This spectacular trophy of the head of the commander was proclaimed throughout the Tokugawa army, and the tide of the battle began to turn their way. Yet still the Osaka army did not give up hope, and in a series of desperate actions almost succeeded in reversing the trend. Ono Harunaga's troops were holding their own against the Tokugawa main body, and if at that moment the rear attack from Akashi had materialised, and Hideyori had sallied out, the course of Japanese history might have been changed. But it was not to be. Akashi was intercepted, and by the time Hideyori ventured out the Tokugawa troops were approaching the moats. Mizuno Katsushige planted his standard on the Sakura gate, and as civilians fled in terror the Tokugawa swarmed into the castle area. Dragging their guns forward the Tokugawa artillery opened up on the keep. The following morning flames were seen. Toyotomi Hideyori had committed suicide, and burned the grand edifice that had once been impregnable.

Chapter 12
CASE STUDY 4: THE CAMPAIGN

For the final case study in the application of the techniques of samurai warfare I have chosen to describe the longest, bitterest, and perhaps the most bloody campaign in samurai history: the eleven-year struggle between Oda Nobunaga and the fanatics of the Ikkō-ikki. It brings out aspects of siege warfare, naval actions and wide-scale samurai combat.

The Revival of the Monk-Soldiers

In a previous chapter it was argued that the military influence of the warrior monks of Kyōto and Nara during the Heian Period and the Nambokuchō Wars was by no means as great as has sometimes been presumed. For the subsequent two centuries little is heard of warriors who combined the profession of arms with that of religion. There are notable exceptions, of course, among individual samurai leaders who, at some stage in their careers, take monastic or priestly vows, such as the illustrious trio of Hōjō Sōun, Takeda Shingen and Uesugi Kenshin, but these are personal gestures, and the men they command are not warrior monks but retained samurai warriors. As the sixteenth century begins we see evidence of a new style of warrior priest arriving on the scene, less monastic and more populist than the Tendai sect Sōhei of Hieizan and Nara. The impression of a social change is the correct one, because the influence of the older Buddhist sects had by then been almost eclipsed by the military strength and the fanaticism of the armies of a very different type of Buddhism, a mass movement which reached the lowest orders of society, and found its military expression through the groups known as the Ikkō-ikki. The second term in the name, 'ikki' strictly means a league, but it has also come to mean a riot, and it was as rioting mobs that the Ikkō-ikki first became known to their samurai betters.

The other word 'Ikkō' provides a clue to their religious affiliation. It means 'single-minded' or 'devoted', and the monto (disciples or adherents of the sect) were completely single-minded in their devotion to Amida, the Supreme Buddha of the Jōdo (Pure Land) in the West, who will welcome all his followers into the paradise of the Pure Land on their death, where they will live in happiness forever. This teaching contrasted sharply with the insistence on the attainment of enlightenment stressed by the older sects. These radical views are particularly associated with the priest Hōnen-Shōnin, born in 1133, who founded the Jōdo sect of Buddhism. The Ikkō-ikki movement derived from a later offshoot of the Jōdo sect, the Jōdo-Shinshū (True Pure Land Sect), founded by Shinran Shōnin (1174–1268) and now Japan's largest Buddhist denomination. Jōdo-Shinshū promised even more immediate salvation; 'Call on the name of Amida and you will be saved' was the cry of the sect's founder. Jōdo Shinshū welcomed all into its fold, and did not insist upon meditation or any intellectual path to salvation. As its clergy were neither required to be celibate nor to withdraw from the world, they were able to evangelise among the peasantry much more freely, and its influence grew rapidly among the common people.

The head of the sect in the fifteenth century was Rennyō (1415–99), who had achieved such fame as a preacher that the rival monks of Mount Hiei had burned his house and forced him to flee north to Kaga province. Here he re-established his headquarters, and very soon his followers became enmeshed in the struggle for supremacy that was going on in Kaga province between various samurai clans. The Ikkō-ikki monto welcomed fighting; their faith promised that paradise was the immediate reward for death in battle, and nothing daunted them. In 1488 Rennyō's Ikkō-ikki revolted against the samurai as a whole, and control of the province of Kaga passed into their hands after a series of fierce skirmishes. For the first time in Japanese history a province was ruled by a group who were neither courtiers nor samurai.

These were heady days for the Ikkō-ikki, and as the fifteenth century drew to its close the sect spread out from Kaga, and established itself in a series of key locations not far from Kyōto. By 1570 there were two major power bases, the Ikkō-ikki fortress of Nagashima, built on a swampy river delta as confusing to strangers as it was powerful, and the greatest Ikkō-ikki centre of all, the huge 'fortified cathedral' of the Ishiyama Honganji. It was built where Osaka castle now stands, and thus threatened the capital from the opposite direction. These main bases, with scores of others, provided the overall organisation for a fanatical army that was to occupy the time and resources of all aspiring samurai generals until 1580.

The Mikawa Monto

We begin our discussion with the Ikkō-ikki of Mikawa province. Several temples, including three in Okazaki: the Shōman-ji, the Jōgu-ji and the Honsō-ji, possessed ikki armies,

Below: The word 'ikki' can also mean a riot, and it was in the form of peasant uprisings that the daimyō first came to experience the fury of the ikki mobs, as in this illustration from the Hōjō Godaiki.

who rubbed shoulders with the territory of the future Shōgun Tokugawa Ieyasu. It was during his successful campaigns against the Mikawa monto that Ieyasu learnt the military skills which were to stand him in such good stead in the years to come. A diorama on display in Okazaki shows priests in full clerical robes with shaven heads, but with some body armour, emerging from the gate of their temple to attack Ieyasu's samurai army. Other illustrations show them as a motley crew, the bulk of their forces clearly being peasants. Their commander, on horseback, is dressed in complete samurai armour, while the equipment of the soldiers on foot ranges from a full Buddhist monk's robes and shaven head, through a peasant's straw rain cloak and foot soldier's jingasa (war hat), to a mix of samurai armour and helmets. Some carry the monk's traditional weapon, the naginata, and prominent are the long nobori (banners) bearing the prayer used by all the Amidist Buddhist sects: 'Namu Amida Butsu' (Hail to the Buddha Amida). This prayer, which was supposedly repeated up to 60,000 times a day by devotees, became the motto of the Ikkō-ikki armies.

Tokugawa Ieyasu's fear was that the Mikawa monto would try to do in his province what Rennyō's men had achieved in Kaga, namely ousting the local daimyō in favour of monastic control. When hostilities first began, Ieyasu's retainer Sakai Tadatsugu wrote to the temples urging them to reflect on the fact that 'Shaving the head and wearing priestly robes is only to put on the outward signs of sanctity, like a bat that pretends to be a bird.' But letters had no effect, and soon the young Ieyasu was engaged in fighting the monk armies at the Battle of Azukizaka in 1564. Not only did they fight under the slogan noted above, but also used a more fanatical banner which, in black ink on a white cloth, declared the conviction that 'He who advances is sure of salvation, but he who retreats will go to hell.' The Ikkō-ikki were well supplied with matchlock muskets, which had only been introduced to Japan some twelve years previously, good evidence of how these monk armies were no longer a peasant rabble, but at the forefront of military technology. Ieyasu took a prominent personal role in the fighting, challenging several of his opponents to single combat, a form of samurai

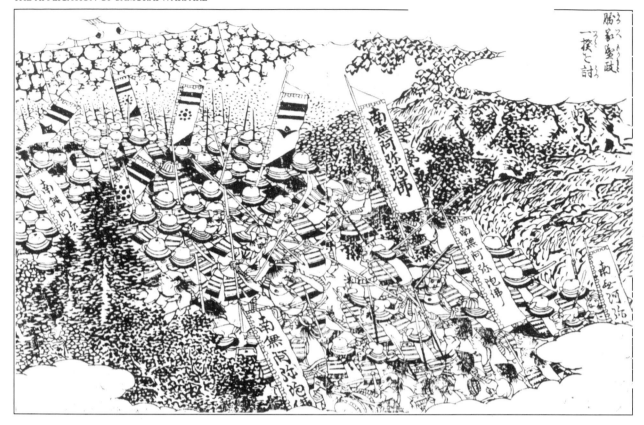

warfare that was rapidly becoming an anachronism. On one charge, with his spear couched like a lance, an arrow struck the reins of his horse, just missing his body. He caught up with his quarry and dealt him two slashing strokes down the back of his armour as he turned to gallop away. On another occasion Ieyasu felt a bullet strike his armour, but thinking that it had not penetrated he fought on, and it was only when he got back to Okazaki castle when the fighting was over that he realised how near he had come to being killed, because when his servant stripped off his body armour two bullets fell out of his shirt.

It was to Ieyasu's great advantage that among the Ikkō-ikki supporters were members of the samurai class who happened to belong to Jōdo-Shinshū, so their loyalties were considerably divided. Some were also vassals of Ieyasu, and at first their religious inclination had made them choose the Ikkō-ikki side in the battle. But as time wore on the traditional samurai loyalty to the lord proved the stronger, and many who changed sides, such as Ishikawa Ienari, were to become Ieyasu's most trusted companions. Needless

to say, such loyalty did not extend down to the peasants who comprised the bulk of the Ikkō-ikki armies. To them all samurai were ultimately enemies to be swept from power in the province.

Ieyasu also benefited from the support given to him by his own particular sect of Buddhism, the Jōdo-shū, the original Amidist sect from which Jōdo-Shinshū had sprung. Jōdo was represented in Okazaki by the Daijū-ji, the temple where all Ieyasu's ancestors were buried. Following the defeat of the Imagawa family, of which he was then a vassal, in 1560 Ieyasu had gone to the Daijū-ji with the intention of committing hara-kiri before the tombs of his ancestors. Toyo, the Chief Priest, managed to dissuade him from this course of action, and presented Ieyasu with a white banner on which was written 'Renounce this filthy world attain the Pure Land', a flag which Ieyasu was to carry with him in all subsequent battles, including ones against the Ikkō-ikki. In 1564 the Daijū-ji sent its own contingent of Jōdo warrior monks to fight for Ieyasu, and with their help the Ikkō-ikki of Mikawa were finally crushed. A subsequent peace

Above: An Ikkō-ikki army on the march. Note the profusion of banners bearing the slogan 'Namu Amida Butsu'.

Above: A book illustration depicting warriors of the Ikkō-ikki marching out of a castle. Their leader is mounted; the others wear a mix of armour. Only one has a shaven head.

conference established that Ieyasu would restore their temples to their original state. This he did with vigour, by burning each one to the ground, arguing to the furious priests that a green field site was the original state!

Oda Nobunaga and the Ikkō-ikki

With the pacification of the Ikkō-ikki of Mikawa, the focus of Ikkō-ikki activity moved westwards to the two centres of Nagashima and Ishiyama Hongan-ji. Compared to the isolated temples of Mikawa, their positions were very strong indeed. Both consisted of a complex series of stockaded fortresses built around a castle and set within a river delta. Nagashima, at the border of Owari and Ise provinces, was located to the south-east of the present-day city of Nagoya, where three rivers, the Kisogawa, the Nagaragawa and the Ibigawa, entered Ise bay, producing a number of islands, reed plains and swamps. The direction of the rivers and the disposition of the islands has continually shifted throughout history, but even today the long, flat island of Nagashima, set among broad rivers and

waving reeds, can easily conjure up the appearance it must have presented to the Ikkō-ikki who garrisoned it during the Sengoku Period.

The central fortress, Nagashima castle, had been built in 1555 by Itō Shigeharu, who lost it to the Ikkō-ikki when he was swept from power in a manner which was becoming only too familiar to daimyō who had this particular variety of rival on their doorstep. As Owari was Oda Nobunaga's home province his family felt the presence of the Nagashima ikki very acutely, and certain members of the Oda clan engaged them in battle at the northern edge of the Nagashima delta at Ogie castle in November 1569. The Ikkō-ikki were completely victorious, and killed Nobunaga's brother Nobuoki. The loss of his brother added a personal dimension to Nobunaga's strategic need to overcome Nagashima, which posed two particular military problems. First, its location controlled the route from Owari province into Ise, and with it the main lines of communication south of Lake Biwa between Nobunaga's secure territories and the capital. Secondly, Nagashima was closely allied with the other main concentration of Ikkō-ikki, who were based on another river delta, and one that was even more formidable than Nagashima. This was the fortress cathedral of Ishiyama Hongan-ji, built where Osaka castle now stands, at the mouth of the Kisogawa at its point of entry to the Inland Sea.

The years between 1570 and 1581 are marked by Oda Nobunaga's greatest achievements towards fulfilling his goal of

Left: This dramatic print is a rare depiction of a warrior monk from the Negoro-ji in Kii province, whose troops were renowned for their firearms skill. His head is shaved, and he wears the monk's robe over a simple suit of armour. He has a naginata in his left hand, and an enormous studded club in his right.

Above: Oda Nobunaga, the hated enemy of the Ikkō-ikki.

one of these quasi-monastic foundations, or to any one of the various other military and religious institutions which provided indirect support to Nagashima and Ishiyama Hongan-ji. These included Ikkō-ikki branches in Kaga and Echizen province, the Saiga temple in Kii province, and a branch of the Nagashima chapter elsewhere in Owari.

Two other allies deserve mention at this stage, for the upsurge in linked religious and military activity had caused something of a revival among the warrior monks of Mount Hiei. No longer were their enemies the temples of Nara. Instead Mount Hiei found its traditional pre-eminence in Kyōto threatened by the growth of another populist Buddhist sect, the Nichiren-shū, named after its founder the monk Nichiren, and otherwise known as the Hokke-shū (Lotus sect), from the importance attached by the believers to the Lotus Sutra. In 1528 the Hokke-shū succeeded in fighting off an attack on Kyōto by the Ikkō-ikki, and then went on the offensive by attacking the Ishiyama Hongan-ji in 1533. The monks of Mount Hiei, thoroughly alarmed by the success of the Hokke-shū, secured the neutrality of local samurai clans and, with the backing of Ishiyama Hongan-ji, raided Kyōto with a ferocity not seen since the Gempei War. Twenty-one Nichiren temples were burned, and much of Kyōto suffered with them. Having rediscovered their military strength, the monks of Mount Hiei sought allies among prominent local samurai. Their location, to the north-east of Kyōto, put them into close proximity to the territories of the Asai and Asakura families, who were Nobunaga's main rivals to the north of the capital, thus threatening his communications to the north of Lake Biwa. So Oda Nobunaga had one further enemy with which to contend.

The other coterie to support the Ikkō-ikki were from the twelfth-century Shingon sect's Negoro temple in Kii province. They are particularly interesting because they were renowned for their use of firearms, and supplied a contingent of gunners to Ishiyama Hongan-ji. They were visited by the European Jesuit missionary Father Caspar Vilela, who has left a fascinating pen-picture of the typical warrior monk army. Being drawn from the esoteric and mystical Shingon sect of Buddhism, whose headquarters lay on the holy mountain of Kōya-

unifying Japan. The decade encompassed the battles of Anegawa and Nagashino, the invasion of Ise and Iga provinces, and the building of Azuchi castle, yet all these campaigns and historic advances were carried out against a background of a continuous threat from, and sporadic war with two huge armies of Ikkō-ikki, one of which was located in Nobunaga's own backyard. Any rival to Nobunaga sought to ally himself to

san, the description of monk-soldiers supposedly owing allegiance to the teachings of the great Kōbō-Daishi comes as something of a surprise. Vilela, of course, was unaware of this religious background, and described the appearance of the Negoro warriors as akin to the Knights of Rhodes. Vilela, however, surmised that most of those he saw had taken no monastic vows, because they wore their hair long, and were devoted to the practice of arms, their monastic rule laying less emphasis on prayer than on military preparation. Each member was required to make five or seven arrows per day, and to practise competitively with bow and matchlock once a week. Their helmets, armour and spears were of astonishing strength, and, to quote Vilela, 'their sharp swords could slice through a man in armour as easily as a butcher carves a tender steak!' Their practice combat with each other was fierce, and the death of one of their number in training was accepted without emotion. Fearless on the battlefield, they enjoyed life off it with none of the restrictions normally associated with the ascetic life, indulging freely in wine, women and, presumably, song.

Nobunaga's first move against the Ishiyama Hongan-ji was launched in August 1570, a few months after his brother's death at Nagashima. He left Gifu castle at the head of 30,000 troops and based himself at Tennōji. With the intention of eventually surrounding the complex he ordered the building of a series of forts around the perimeter, but on 12 September the bells rang out at midnight from within the Ishiyama Hongan-ji headquarters, and two of Nobunaga's fortresses, at Kawaguchi and Takadono, were attacked. The Oda army were stunned both by the ferocity of the surprise attack, and also by the novel use of controlled volley firing from 3,000 matchlockmen. This little-known battle predates the famous Battle of Nagashino by five years, and was probably the first example of organised volleyed musket fire used in battle in Japan. In the chronicle Shinchōkōki we read that 'the enemy gunfire echoed between heaven and earth', resulting in the withdrawal of the Oda main body, leaving a handful of forts to attempt the task of monitoring, if not controlling, the mighty fortress of Ishiyama Hongan-ji. It was a process that would take eleven years and much of Nobunaga's military resources, in

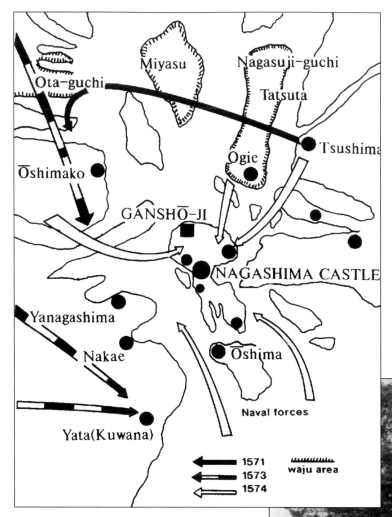

the first long-term campaign to be seen in Japanese history.

The Defence of Nagashima

The shock provided by the Ishiyama Hongan-ji forced Nobunaga to turn his attentions to Nagashima. The name 'Nagashima' is believed to derive from 'Nana shima'('the seven islands') which, with a host of smaller ones, filled the delta. There were effectively two key areas in Nagashima's defences: Nagashima castle, and the fortified monastery of Ganshō-ji.

Nobunaga's success against the Asai and the Asakura at the battle of the Anegawa had ensured that his northern flanks would remain quiet for at least a few months during 1571. He appointed as commanders of the Nagashima force his trusted generals Sakuma Nobumori and Shibata Katsuie. The Nagashima defenders, relying on the reports

Left: Map showing Oda Nobunaga's three campaigns against the Ikkō-ikki of Nagashima.

Below: The Ganshō-ji, Nagashima, which still bears the appearance of a fortified monastery.

they had heard of the action at the Ishiyama Hongan-ji, made suitable preparations, strengthening their outposts and setting up various defensive measures. On 16 May 1571 Nobunaga's army pitched camp at Tsushima, to the north-east of Nagashima, which was divided from the complex by a broad but particularly shallow river. An attack was planned on the area immediately to the west of Tsushima against the series of wajū (island communities protected by dikes against flooding), from where an attack could be launched on the Ganshō-ji. Nobunaga's mounted samurai began to ford towards the first wajū, only to find that the river bottom consisted of deep mud. The horses were soon bogged down, and as they struggled many threw off their heavily armoured riders, who were met by a hail of arrows and bullets, causing severe casualties. As the survivors dragged themselves to the nearest dry land, the wajū of Nagasuji-guchi, they encountered ropes stretched between stakes, which further hindered

their progress towards safety. The shoreline was covered by tall, dense reeds, which acted as a magnet to the desperate and demoralised samurai. As they crawled into the reedbeds they discovered them to be swarming with more Ikkō-ikki gunners and archers, who cut them down like flies. The shores of the reedbeds were also booby-trapped by the simple addition of old pots and vases, buried up to the necks in the sand, providing a trap for ankles, and further reducing the samurai withdrawal to a sitting target.

As night fell the defenders realised that the sole survivors of the Oda army were confined within the next wajū of Ota-guchi, so the dike was cut, rapidly flooding the low-lying land, catching the remaining samurai in an inrush of muddy water. Nobunaga's first attack on Nagashima had been an unmitigated disaster. General Shibata Katsuie had been severely wounded, and no impression had been made against the defences. As the Oda army withdrew they

THE BOMBARDMENT OF OSAKA CASTLE IN 1614

Artillery played a decisive part in the Winter Campaign of Osaka in 1614/15. Here the two brothers Tokugawa Hidetada and Tokugawa Yoshinao discuss the progress of the siege from the artillery lines, which look out through the morning mist across the frozen ground to the towers of Osaka castle in the distance. No less than 300 heavy guns kept up the pressure on the Osaka garrison during the winter months.

Hidetada, Tokugawa Ieyasu's heir, and overall commander during the siege, is wearing a fairly simple armour of a ni-mai-dō laced in kebiki style with blue cords. The helmet also is a plain design of black-lacquered iron with a small central ridge. The actual armour is preserved in the Kunozan Tōshōgū Museum in Shizuoka. By way of contrast with Hidetada's years of experience on the battlefield, his brother Yoshinao, who was Tokugawa Ieyasu's seventh son, received his first taste of combat at Osaka at the age of fifteen. Like Hidetada he is wearing a sombre armour of black lacquer, but his is also laced in black. The helmet and face mask are a striking addition to the ensemble. The helmet has a distinctive black catfish tail bowl, with a plume of feathers mounted at the rear. His armour is preserved in the Tokugawa Art Museum in Nagoya. The nearest gunners are operating sakers, mounted on a wooden framework and elevated by a series of ropes. Support for the culverins to the rear is provided by rice-straw bags stuffed with sand. The lines are protected from surprise attack by wooden and bamboo palisades and earthworks. The officers in charge of the artillery crews wear quilted cotton haori (surcoats) over their armour to ward off the winter cold. One uses a telescope – obtained, no doubt, from a Dutch trader.

burned several villages on the outskirts, which probably had no effect other than inclining the sympathies of the local population more towards the cause of their monastic neighbours.

As 1571 wore on, the potential danger from the Asai and Asakura began to look more acute, so Nobunaga decided on a course of action which would be as much a symbolic gesture towards the Ikkō-ikki and their allies as of military significance. In battle terms, Nobunaga chose the soft target of Mount Hiei, where there were no swamps or river to hinder his advance, and the ruthlessness with which it was pursued sent shock waves through the other monk-soldier confraternities. During the campaigns of 1570 Mount Hiei had provided sanctuary and support for the Asai and Asakura families, but had seen its monk army easily defeated in battle by Nobunaga's General Toyotomi Hideyoshi. Despite the now

reduced threat, Nobunaga decided to burn down the entire temple complex as a precaution and a warning.

The assault began on 29 September 1571. Nobunaga first burned the town of Sakamoto, at the foot of Mount Hiei, but most of the townspeople had taken refuge on the mountain. He took particular care to destroy the Hiyoshi shrine of the Kami Sannō, the Mountain King, and then deployed his 30,000 men in a vast ring around the mountain. A conch trumpet sounded and the troops began to move steadily upwards, burning anything in their way and killing men, women and children. By nightfall the main temple of Enryaku-ji had gone up in flames, and many monks had leapt into the fire. Next day Nobunaga sent his gunners out to pursue any who had escaped. The final casualty list probably topped 20,000, and was the end of the long history of the warrior monks of the Tendai sect's temples of Mount Hiei. In time the monks returned and rebuilt, but never again would they take the field as monk armies.

Following this overwhelming success, Nobunaga reduced a minor Ikkō-ikki outpost within Owari province by leading the defenders out on the basis of a spurious peace treaty, and massacring them where they stood. The defenders of Nagashima may have been horrified by the attack on Mount Hiei and the fate of their companions in Owari, but they were neither discouraged nor intimidated, and when Nobunaga turned his attentions for a second time to Nagashima the Ikkō-ikki had once again made careful plans. The campaign began in July 1573 and this time Nobunaga took personal charge of the operations. The numbers of his army are not recorded, but we do know that he recruited heavily from Ise province. His army also contained a well-drilled matchlock corps, demonstrating that Nobunaga could learn from past experience. Avoiding the obstacles encountered in 1571, and covered by an advance from the west under Sakuma Nobumori and Hashiba (later Toyotomi) Hideyoshi, Nobunaga sent his gunners on ahead along the main roads into Nagashima, hoping that volley fire would blast a way for him. Unfortunately for Nobunaga, as soon as his men were ready to fire, a fierce downpour occurred, and the rain soaked the matches and the pans, ren-

dering nine out of every ten arquebuses temporarily inoperable. The Ikkō-ikki took it as a sign from heaven of divine favour, and launched an immediate counter-attack for which the forward matchlockmen were ill prepared. They began to fall back, taking the Ise troops with them, and as the Ikkō-ikki pressed forward they received a further sign from heaven as the clouds parted and the rain stopped, enabling them to use their own matchlocks, whose pans had been closed and whose fuses were in dry bags. The defenders advanced perilously close to Nobunaga himself, who was in the thick of the fighting astride a horse. One bullet narrowly missed his ear, and another felled one of his retainers who was shot through the armpit. For the second time in two years, the Oda army withdrew, hearing on the wind the sound of a mass chanting of 'Namu Amida Butsu' as the Ikkō-ikki gave thanks for their further salvation from the 'Devil Nobunaga'. The western force had been more successful. Takigawa Kazumasu took Yata castle (the present-day Kuwana) which was the most southerly point of the

Nagashima complex, but a counter-attack forced him to withdraw.

Nobunaga returned to the fray for a third time in 1574, but he was now much better armed. His conquest of Ise, though hindered by the Nagashima campaign, had brought to his side an unusual naval talent in the person of Kuki Yoshitaka (1542–1600), a man who, like many of the Japanese sea captains of his day, had once been a successful pirate, operating around Ise bay and the Kii peninsula. Nobunaga recruited Kuki and his fleet to take the fight by ship close to the Ikkō-ikki fortifications in a way that had never proved possible before. Kuki's erstwhile pirates kept up a rolling bombardment of the Nagashima defences from close on shore, concentrating on the wooden watchtowers with cannonballs and fire arrows.

The presence of the ships also served to cut off the garrison from supplies and from any possible relieving force; more crucially, they enabled Nobunaga's land-based troops to take most of the Ikkō-ikki's outlying forts. Two in particular, Nakae and Yanagashima, enabled Nobunaga to control access from the

Above: This gateway is all that remains of Nagashima castle, centre of the Nagashima Ikkō-ikki defences.

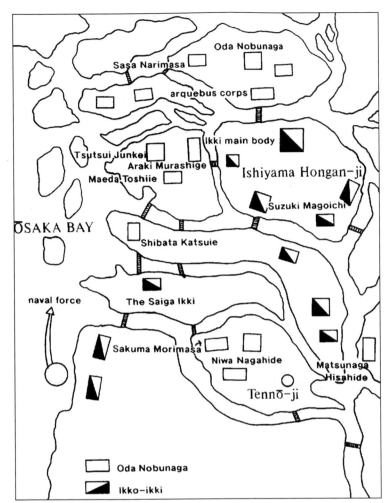

Oda Nobunaga
Saśa Narimasa
arquebus corps
Tsutsui Junkei
Ikki main body
Araki Murashige
Maeda Toshiie
Ishiyama Hongan-ji
Suzuki Magoichi
ŌSAKA BAY
Shibata Katsuie
naval force
The Saiga Ikki
Sakuma Morimasa
Niwa Nagahide
Matsunaga Hisahide
Tennō-ji

☐ Oda Nobunaga

◣ Ikko-ikki

Above: Map showing Oda Nobunaga's campaign against the Ishiyama Hongan-ji.

crammed into the inner outposts. Unseen by them, Nobunaga had mountainous piles of dry brushwood stacked against the palisade. He waited for the strong winds that heralded the approach of the September typhoons (to which Ise bay is prone), and set light to the massive pyre. Burning brands jumped the small gaps of water, and soon the whole of the Nagashima complex was ablaze. As at Mount Hiei, no mercy was shown, but at Nagashima none was asked for, because the flatlands provided no resistance to the fierce fires, and all 20,000 inhabitants of the Ikkō-ikki fortress were burned to death before any could escape to be cut down.

Thus ended one of the most protracted and most brutal of all Nobunaga's campaigns. As noted earlier, the overall atmosphere of Nagashima today is still able to evoke impressions of the sixteenth century. The land is flat. Much of it is reclaimed, and the rice fields are bordered by reedbeds as they reach the shore. One gate and part of the moat is all that remains of Nagashima castle, which Nobunaga presented to Takigawa Kazumasu in 1574 as a reward, for it was he who had captured it temporarily in 1573. Its keep survived until 1959 when it was struck by lightning. Typhoons have caused their own deprivations. Having lost its original location to the sea, the Ganshō-ji has been rebuilt farther inland, and still boasts a stone wall which gives it the appearance of a fortified place. Within its courtyard is the most interesting feature of all: a stone stupa erected recently as a memorial to the martyrs of the Ikkō-ikki, who held Nagashima for four years against the mightiest military power then known in Japan.

The Fall of the Ishiyama Hongan-ji

With the destruction of Nagashima the fortress cathedral of Ishiyama Hongan-ji stood alone. Like Nagashima, it was built upon a series of islands on a river delta, but, unlike Nagashima, the river did not open out on to the wide Ise Bay, but on to the narrow Inland Sea, which was largely controlled by the fleet of Nobunaga's deadly enemies, the Mōri clan.

By 1576 the main building of Ishiyama Hongan-ji had become the centre of a complex ring of 51 outposts, well supported by organised firearms squads. At the beginning of that year Nobunaga was preoccupied with building his magnificent castle of Azuchi and

western, Ise side, for the first time. Supported by Kuki, a land-based army carried out a three-pronged attack from the north. Gradually the defenders were forced back, though with enormous resistance, and were squeezed down into the small area of the island on which stood the fortified Ganshō-ji and Nagashima castle, with little else in the way of territory, and almost no hope of relief. By the end of August 1574 they were slowly starving to death, and ready to talk peace, but their overtures fell on deaf ears. Mindful of the death of his brother, and his own humiliation at their hands, Nobunaga resolved to destroy the islands of Nagashima as thoroughly as he had destroyed Mount Hiei. Instead of accepting surrender, he built a very tall wooden palisade which was anchored on the forts of Nakae and Yanagashima, and which physically isolated the Ikkō-ikki from the gaze of the outside world. Approximately 20,000 people were now

149

Japan enjoyed a winter break from fighting, but in April he returned to warlike activities and made a land-based attack on the Ishiyama Hongan-ji with a force of 3,000 men under the command of Araki Muneshige and Akechi Mitsuhide. This may have been more of an exercise in testing the defenders' mettle, because 15,000 men were pitted against him, and Nobunaga was forced to withdraw. In May he carried out another attack, known as the Battle of Mitsuji, a fierce skirmish provoked by the mass chanting of the nenbutsu ('Namu Amida Butsu') from the defenders. Nobunaga was personally involved in the hand-to- hand combat, and led a contingent of ashigaru in a sally that drove the Ikkō-ikki back to one of their inner gates. Nobunaga received a bullet wound in his leg before he withdrew.

The ferocity of the defence forced Nobunaga to revise his tactics, and he changed his immediate aim to that of reducing the outposts of the Ishiyama Hongan-ji, thus progressively isolating the centre. In a series of campaigns he destroyed the Ikkō-ikki outpost of Saiga in Kii province to the south, who had been able to support the fortress from the sea and had been present at

Nagashima. For good measure he sent Toyotomi Hideyoshi against the other hornets' nest of warrior monks at Negoro in Kii province, now much weakened by the defeat of Nagashima. Negoro-ji was not defeated in this attack (Hideyoshi eventually crushed them in 1585), but was sufficiently contained so as not to cause much of a threat to Nobunaga's immediate plans. With outside forces reduced to a minimum, Nobunaga began what was to develop into a four-year siege, trying to isolate and confine Ishiyama Hongan-ji as he had Nagashima. Nobunaga once again enlisted the services of his admiral, Kuki Yoshitaka, to enforce the blockade by sea, but, unlike the Nagashima situation, a rival fleet in the shape of the Mōri clan navy was willing to challenge him. In August 1576 Mōri demonstrated his superiority by breaking Nobunaga's blockade of the Ishiyama Hongan-ji at the Battle of Kizugawaguchi.

Despite Nobunaga's ineffective blockade, it soon became clear to the defenders that there were no more Ikkō sympathisers left to come and join them. The evident loss of this support alarmed the Ishiyama Hongan-ji, and the Abbot Kōsa sent desperate requests

Above: The monks of the Jōdo sect's Daijū-ji temple in Okazaki help Tokugawa Ieyasu defeat the Ikkō-ikki of Mikawa province. On the right is the flag 'Renounce this filthy world and attain the Pure Land' presented to Ieyasu by the temple. In front of Ieyasu's horse stands Honda Tadakatsu, with deer antlers on his helmet. To the rear, in brown helmet, is Watanabe Hanzō. The woodblock print is by Yoshitoshi.

for help throughout the country. Many Ikkō-ikki branches were already represented within the castle, but no others came to join them, and in 1578 the tide of the siege began to move Nobunaga's way. The 'iron ships' cut Mōri's supply line for good. Now completely isolated, the fanatics of the Ishiyama Hongan-ji prepared to face Nobunaga's final assault, but astonishingly the siege still had two years left to run. The garrison were under the spirited command of a certain Shimotsuma Nakayuki (1551–1616), who was a priest of the Ikkō-ikki as well as a samurai general. In more confident days it had been the intention of the Ishiyama Hongan-ji to march on the capital and make Shimotsuma the new Shōgun, but it had become clear that their support was now coming only from within their own sectarian ranks. No samurai clan had responded to their call to arms, and Uesugi Kenshin, who had threatened Nobunaga from the north and supported the Hongan-ji, died in 1578. His death was so convenient for Nobunaga that ninja were suspected. The Mōri clan were also unwilling to engage in a full-scale struggle with their rival, so the Ishiyama Hongan-ji became progressively weakened, just as Nobunaga had planned. The final straw for the Mōri was the loss of their strategic castle of Miki in 1580, thus depriving them of a convenient base for supporting the Ishiyama Hongan-ji.

Dressed in a sombre suit of armour, and under a red banner with an enormous golden sun's disc, the commander Shimotsuma directed his operations as Nobunaga's

armies whittled at the outer lines of his defences. Every day the attacks continued, using up the cathedral's precious ammunition. Very soon Shimotsuma's food supplies also began to dry up, and Mōri and his fleet could not move from port to aid them. A conference was held by Abbot Kōsa and his colleagues, and in April 1580 an Imperial Messenger was sent with a letter from no less a person than the Emperor of Japan, suggesting an honourable surrender. The letter had of course been prompted by Oda Nobunaga, but it did the trick, and the fortress surrendered a few weeks later. The actual surrender terms, which were bloodless, were accepted by Kōsa's son, and eleven years of bitter fighting came to an end in August 1580. Despite the precedents he had set on Mount Hiei and at Nagashima, Nobunaga acted with uncharacteristic generosity towards the sect that had caused him so much trouble. The castle complex was burned down, but Shimotsuma Nakayuki, who had signed a written oath in his own blood, was spared his life, and in a remarkable gesture was presented by his colleagues with a small statue of Amida Buddha in recognition of his services.

The long story of the warrior monks was, however, not quite over. Abbot Kōsa sought every opportunity to restore the cathedral of the sect, but only as the religious headquarters of Jōdo Shinshū, and not as a fortress. After Nobunaga's death Kōsa petitioned his successor, Toyotomi Hideyoshi, for support. It was granted after Kōsa sent some of the

Below: The attack on the Ishiyama Hongan-ji as depicted in a print by Chikafusa.

few remaining Ikkō-ikki warriors to harass Shibata Katsuie's rear during the Shizugatake campaign in 1583. In gratitude to the warrior monks, Hideyoshi made a parcel of land available in Kyōto in 1589, and the headquarters were rebuilt in 1591. Other religious contingents fared less well. The monks of Negoro did not petition Hideyoshi for support, but instead very unwisely supported his rival during the Komaki campaign of 1584. This folly brought terrible retribution upon them the following year. Their skill with firearms was still considerable, requiring Hideyoshi to bring a matchlock corps of 7,000 against them, but the result was the total destruction of the Negoro complex, in as thorough a job as Nobunaga had performed on Mount Hiei.

The final settlement of the Ikkō-ikki problem can be seen by any visitor to Kyōto today. On leaving the station one is struck by the fact that there are two Jōdo-Shinshū temples called the Nishi Hongan-ji and the Higashi Hongan-ji, both of which appear to be the headquarters of the same organisation, and which are built almost next to each other. The explanation is that in 1602 Tokugawa Ieyasu, who had himself suffered at the hands of the Mikawa monto, took advantage of a succession dispute among the Jōdo-Shinshū and founded an alternative head temple to rival the existing one built by Hideyoshi in 1591. This weakened the political power of the sect, leaving it as a strong religious organisation, but never again capable of becoming the monk army of the Ikkō-ikki.

The greatest compliment that any samurai leader was to pay to the Ikkō-ikki had already been given by Toyotomi Hideyoshi. He had recognised that the site of Ishiyama Hongan-ji was a superb strategic and defensive location. Recalling how it had frustrated his master for so long, he chose it as the site for his main castle that was to become the centre of the great city of Osaka.

Right: A major theme running through the entire history of samurai warfare is the importance attached to loyalty. This hanging scroll is an unusual depiction of the paragons of loyalty, the Forty-Seven Loyal Retainers of Ako, otherwise known as the Forty-Seven Rōnin. (Courtesy of Christie's)

EPILOGUE

Apart from the short-lived Shimabara Rebellion of 1638, the fall of Osaka castle marked the end of samurai warfare. It was almost inevitable that the fighting skill of the samurai should then decline through lack of use. The Shōgun Tokugawa Yoshimune, who reigned from 1716 to 1745, made a valiant attempt to revive the martial accomplishments of his ancestors. Mock battles and manoeuvres were conducted on the plains below Mount Fuji, while enthusiastic daimyō such as the Matsuura of Hirado attempted to apply the latest in military thinking to their own peacetime armies.

Yamaga Sokō, the inspiration for the Matsuura, was also one of the founders of the military theory known as bushidō (the way of the warrior). Yamaga's most celebrated pupil was Oishi Yoshio, who led the famous raid of the Forty-Seven Loyal Retainers of Ako in 1702. Their master was required to perform certain duties at the Shōgun's Court. He received instruction in etiquette from a samurai named Kira who, being dissatisfied by the presents Asano gave him for the lessons, missed no opportunity to ridicule his pupil. One day Asano could take the insults no longer, drew his wakizashi (short sword) and wounded Kira in the head. Even to draw a weapon within the Shōgun's palace was a very serious offence, and Asano was made to commit hara-kiri. His retainers were now dispossessed, and swore revenge. The extraordinary feature to their vengeance is the great lengths they went to in order to keep the plans secret. Their leader, Oishi Yoshio, even descended into drunken debauchery to make Kira think they had forgotten their dead master and his cause. One snowy night they assembled, donned the odd bits of armour they had collected, and attacked Kira's mansion. They overcame the guards, killed Kira and took his head which they laid on Asano's tomb. Their action placed the authorities in a dilemma. Should they punish the forty-six (one had died during the attack), or reward them for behaving like the true samurai the government wished to revive? In the end the law prevailed, and the men committed suicide. Their graves in the Sengaku-ji in Tokyo are a place of 'samurai pilgrimage' to this day

The exploit of the 'Forty-Seven Rōnin' was one piece of evidence that the samurai spirit was dormant rather than extinct. Further evidence was provided in the 1850s and 1860s when Japan was opening up to the outside world. Many samurai wanted to resist the West, and felt the Shōgun was betraying Japan by signing treaties with America and Britain. These clans favoured a restoration of the Emperor, and to bring it about they themselves courted the foreigners to obtain modern weapons from them. The result was a bloody civil war. The Tokugawa Shōgun was deposed in 1868, and Emperor Meiji took back the power his ancestors had granted to Minamoto Yoritomo in 1192. But there was no looking back for Japan. In 1876 the wearing of swords was banned to all but the members of Japan's new conscript army. If a samurai were not an army officer his days as a swordsman were over. One samurai, Saigo Takamori, found it too much to bear, and led an army of followers in the Satsuma Rebellion. They fought as bravely as the samurai of old, but they were no match for modern rifles and cannon. Saigo Takamori ended his life in grand style by committing hara-kiri. He was the last of the samurai.

The preceding pages have shown the fine detail of both the myth and the reality of samurai warfare. There were enormous technological and social developments between the time of the Heian bushi and the Tokugawa ashigaru, but through its long history samurai warfare cherished certain very consistent themes as dearly as it cherished its myths. Fundamental to it was the notion of the élite nature of the samurai warrior. Closely related to this attitude was the value attached to individual prowess, such as the almost reverential awe reserved for the samurai who was the first into battle.

In tension with the demands of individual glory we find the great value attached to support within a defined group, be it family, vassals or allies. The skilled commander had therefore to balance his army's activities at three levels: the person, the group and the army. As armies also involved alliances between clans, it seems amazing that battles were ever fought to order, let alone won to it. The demands of honour and glory had always to be matched against a need for surprise, or the equally demanding virtue of patience during a long siege. In such trying circumstances, samurai tradition was stretched to its limits.

Thus wooden castles were replaced by stone ones; long spears replaced naginata, disciplined infantry replaced the mob, and matchlocks replaced bows, but somehow the man remained the same. Emperor Tenmu had tried to replace private armies by conscripts, but the system was abandoned after a century. Throughout the next millennium nothing could replace the samurai, until the example of contemporary European warfare abolished the class and the concept overnight, in favour of a conscript arrangement of which Emperor Tenmu would have approved. Until then the ideals of samurai warfare blended happily with the reality of its expression, in a military system that was at times efficient, at times romantic, and always unique.

Left: Colour-guards of the Matsuura army for the four hata-jirushi banners.

Left: The side ranks of the Matsuura army: missile weapons and spears.

INDEX AND GLOSSARY